Past Lives, Present Loves

JEANNE AVERY

A SIGNET VISIONS BOOK

SIGNET
Published by New American Library, a division of
Penguin Putnam Inc., 375 Hudson Street,
New York, New York 10014, U.S.A.
Penguin Books Ltd, 27 Wrights Lane,
London W8 5TZ, England
Penguin Books Australia Ltd,
Ringwood, Victoria, Australia
Penguin Books Canada Ltd, 10 Alcorn Avenue,
Toronto, Ontario, Canada M4V 3B2
Penguin Books (N.Z.) Ltd, 182–190 Wairau Road,
Auckland 10, New Zealand

Penguin Books Ltd, Registered Offices:
Harmondsworth, Middlesex, England

First published by Signet, an imprint of New American Library,
a division of Penguin Putnam Inc.

First Printing, September 1999
10 9 8 7 6 5 4 3 2 1

Material on pp. 66–75 is from *A Soul's Journey* by Jeanne Avery, copyright ©
1996 by Jeanne Avery. Used by permission of Boru Books.
Material on pp. 131–157 is from *Astrology and Your Past Lives* by Jeanne Avery,
copyright © 1987 by Jeanne Avery. Reprinted with permission of Fireside, an
imprint of Simon & Schuster.

 REGISTERED TRADEMARK—MARCA REGISTRADA

Printed in the United States of America

CONTENTS

1. Love makes the world go 'round.
   Reincarnation and present-life attractions.   1
2. Regression therapy; how it heals
   problematic relationships in the present.   21
3. Eternal love; back together again.   45
4. Past-life separations; present-day
   frustrations.   55
5. Past-life violence; fears and repression
   in the present.   111
6. Past-life jealousy and passion; separation
   in the present.   131
7. Past-life debts or obligation; financial
   conditions now.   159
8. Past-life abuse; sexual problems now.   179
9. Past-life betrayal; present-life antagonism.   203
10. Change of race from life to life.   223
11. How to conduct self-regression;
    rectifying past mistakes.   237

To Juan de Aguirre and Susan Strasberg, my dearest friends, recently departed from the earth plane, but always very close to me in my conscious mind.

To Swami Chakradhari, with deep eternal love. Each morning, while writing this book, I was awakened at 5:00 A.M. A tremendous jolt of energy switched on my mind and propelled me to the computer. I knew, with certainty, that Swami was saying his prayers and included me in the process. For that powerful healing I am truly grateful.

CHAPTER 1

Love makes the world go 'round. Reincarnation and present-life attractions.

When the first delicate flower of love begins to bloom, excitement permeates the air, hearts beat faster, and the world, in general, looks bright and beautiful. Unfortunately, many relationships that hold so much promise in the beginning can begin to tarnish, in time, like silver that has been neglected. A lovely lady from South America asked, "Why didn't my husband show his true personality before we were married? He is so different now, I'm thinking of getting a divorce."

It is often the case that men and women are so eager to put their own best foot forward in a new relationship, they overlook the very traits and habits in another person that can bring later discomfort. Daughters swear they will never make the same mistakes in love and marriage that their mothers made. But they can easily end up in a similar situation without recognizing the pattern before it is too late. Sons may become so enraptured by a sexual challenge, they seem to be oblivious to anything else. They can suffer deeply when the realization dawns that they are stuck in a relationship lacking in communication, as an example. Why is it that all matters connected to love can be so complicated, when that one area of life might, hopefully, provide a warm blanket of security and feelings of happiness?

Throughout time, fairly simplistic messages about love and relationships are conveyed to the young. "Boy meets girl; boy and girl fall in love; boy and girl marry, have children, and live happily ever after." A revised modern-day script might read, "Boy and girl meet, boy and girl are sexually attracted, live together, marry (or not), have children (or not), face their conflicts, and either decide to work it out or part forever." Yet romance novels still weave spells of alluring fantasies about long-haired, modern-day, bare-chested knights in blue jeans sweeping young women off their feet.

Love stories focused on a more realistic view of romance during the years of World War II, when movie themes reflected difficult times. Tales of anguished young lovers being torn from each other's arms, with nothing to assure them of a future life together, formed the basis of many movie scripts. Hollywood productions of today continue to delve deeply into the tragedy of love lost, the joy of love found, and the sadness of love missed. But few scripts give answers as to why conflicts or sadness should be inherent in love relationships.

Ralph Waldo Emerson wrote, " 'Tis better to have loved and lost, than not to love at all." As the world prepares to enter the twenty-first century, it appears this sentiment still holds true, in some instances. Occasionally, the public hears of real-life stories of true love. Actions echo more loudly than any words, when we learn of personal sacrifice from those people who truly and deeply love another. We are profoundly touched when we see Ekatarina Gordieff, the beautiful young widow of Sergei Grinkov, perform alone on ice. Shining through her graceful and beautiful skating is the ever-present sadness about her Sergei. She dances the constant deep love she feels for him, but as she swirls over the ice, her empty arms convey the aching pain she feels over her loss. We wonder why such love between two people couldn't last a lifetime.

Emerson also wrote, "Love and you shall be loved; All love is mathematically just, as much as the two sides of an algebraic equation." Loss such as that of Ekaterina's, among many other such real-life stories of sad loss, hardly seems just, and daily accounts of abuse in relationships seen on television and read in the news makes Emerson's concept even more difficult to accept. Love doesn't seem to be fair at all.

The current trend on television talk shows in the United States is to allow angry people to air their more intimate secrets of relationships gone wrong. Hosts guide their guests through bizarre and anguished stories of abuse and violence. Sometimes these people actually come to blows before the eyes of the camera and the whole world.

We read many sensationalized reports of conflicts

between couples that hardly seem fair. It often appears that one person loves more than another. That person may, indeed, become victimized. When violence first begins to take place in what was formerly a harmonious relationship, why don't the victims simply walk away? Why would one partner be willing to take whatever is dished out and become a punching bag for the other? What keeps people together in an abusive situation? Tragically, the accounts of unrest and disagreements appear to be increasing, as millions of words are written or spoken in all forms of media that depict man's inhumanity to man. Even worse are the methods people employ to get even with each other, thereby continuing the original conflict. The crimes that are committed in the name of love are hardly just and fair.

As the mystery of attractions and rejections between the sexes continues to be a prime topic of discussion in the media, attempts are made to provide some solution to these problems. Articles appear in magazines, TV, and publications describing new techniques that relate to the age-old battle between the sexes. But misconduct continues unabated in spite of therapy, open discussions, and confrontations. We seem to be making little headway in finding final answers.

In the 1800s poets wrote about love above all else. Alfred Lord Tennyson said, "In the Spring a young man's fancey lightly turns to thoughts of love." But Lord George Gordon Byron took a sexist view when he wrote, "Man's love is of man's life a part; it is woman's whole existence." Perhaps Walt Whitman was more profound when he confessed, "I could never explain why I love anybody, or anything."

As life becomes more complicated, people are encouraged to speak out to tell the truth about what goes on in the privacy of their homes. Complex relationships that were formerly kept under wraps are emerging into daylight. Princess Diana broke new ground when she appeared on television and told the truth about her unhappy marriage. Among other things, she revealed that Prince Charles spent the night before their wedding with his true love, Camilla.

It had long been established in royal circles that men were allowed to have a mistress, but that women were not to take lovers. And no one was expected to reveal inside information to anyone beyond the intimate circle of the royals. It took courage on Diana's part to tell the truth about the pain she felt over Charles' infidelities and even more honesty to reveal the truth about her own extramarital affairs. But her confessions came years too late to rectify the hurtful interactions and heal the widening breach between the warring prince and princess. Much of the bad press and misunderstandings about Diana might have been explained from the beginning, if the public had known of the intense pain that accompanied her awareness of Charles' love for Camilla. His original infidelity overshadowed any chance for their love to flourish. How tragic that Diana died just as it appeared she might have found some emotional happiness with a new love in her life. Research reveals that as much unhappiness existed between royal couples in days of old as in current times. Princess Diana was able to tell the world about an unhappy, loveless marriage whereas Anne Boleyn could never tell the populace about her intimate relationship with Henry VIII. Anne might have had some clues about her future with Henry when he was so eager to recount to the courts all that was wrong with his first marriage. Eventually, Henry was quite vocal about his displeasure with Anne. Poor Anne probably had no choice but to marry Henry, even with dire portents about her future. We cannot know what her misgivings might have been.

Elizabeth Taylor and Richard Burton had a fairy-tale story of love and romance. Even though two other people were terribly hurt by Liz and Dick's desire to be together, the public accepted them as the newest princess and knight in shining armor, with hardly a backward glance at Eddie and Sybil. Eventually private battles between Liz and Dick became public knowledge. Even with a divorce and remarriage, basic problems could not be overcome. The blazing light of love dimmed to a tiny flicker. They even continued to torture each other long after the final divorce when they were together again in a Broadway production and tour of *Separate Tables*. Backstage rumors had it that Liz would take a swig of whiskey before her biggest love scene with Richard, who, as a recovering alcoholic, was on the wagon. In such closeness, he was forced to smell the liquor on her breath.

What is it about love and relationships that can remain so elusive? Why is it that true, undying, long-lasting love is so rare? Why is it that deep, passionate, romantic love is so often accompanied by tragedy? How is it that the sweetest romance on earth can often be so short-lived? It would seem that with all the available information about relationships, the most important concern couples might have before they make a commitment is the guarantee of happiness. How can we know in advance that an attraction will last and be loving throughout time? Couples seem to accept, as a matter of fact, that love may present problems that defy easy solution. The subject of a recent television show was "How to survive the first year of marriage." Is it possible that men and women need information even from the very beginning of a loving partnership?

It would be hopeful to think that the first days of togetherness would be smooth, problem free, and private. What happens to the attractions, flirtations, and wooing that helps two people come together? Why can't we teach our young about the steps to take to insure a solid foundation for a relationship? Why do we allow reluctant commitment to be the premise for an involvement with another being? So far no one seems to have the answers. But we cannot live with love or without it.

A by-product of all the exposure about relationships is a fear of commitment to one long-term relationship. But even before a couple can progress to the stage of taking a first step, there can be difficulty

Jeanne Avery

meeting someone to love. Walls of fear prevent a natural attraction to take hold on a normal, step-by-step basis. People no longer seem to trust their own instincts about each other. They often look to experts to guide them through the mine field of growing fondness. No course in school has yet been devised to prepare young people for the most important times of their lives.

The story of men and women has not progressed very far from the days of Adam and Eve. Eve refused to listen, and look what happened. Do you think Adam was angry about losing paradise? Do you think he might have reminded Eve of her mistake on a regular basis?

Periodically someone comes up with a new system of personality analysis in an attempt to help people understand each other. Recently, a new way of relating personality types to colors seems to help people identify themselves and others. Without very much training, one could imagine that a "red" person will be impatient, innovative, pioneering, competitive, and energetic. A "blue" person might be calm and concerned about fair play. A "yellow" person is sunny, sociable, and happy. This may give some kind of guidance about why personality conflicts emerge, but in the final analysis, the method may be too simplistic to be of real help if major conflicts already exist.

The Myers-Briggs Type Indicator was developed by two women, Katharine Briggs and her daughter Isabel Briggs Myers. Mrs. Briggs became an exhaus-

8

tive student of Carl Jung's works and, with her daughter, set out to design a psychological instrument that would explain, in rigorous scientific terms, the difference in personality types according to Jung's Theory of Personality Preferences. The idea behind the MBTI was that it could be used to establish individual preferences, and then to promote a more constructive use of the differences between people. The idea continues to stress that much of a person's attraction toward specific people in your life is the result of your personality preferences. By understanding some underlying patterns, two people can qualify where similarities and differences make for harmony and where they can cause discord.

A deeper understanding and appreciation of another person can be developed through identifying underlying patterns of communications. NLP (Neurolinguistic Programming) is a method of identification that can help eliminate some misunderstandings in intimate situations, by making sure that messages are received and processed accurately. With a little bit of effort and some basic skills, each person in a relationship can greatly enhance an ability to express themselves in a way that their partner can comprehend the true thought being expressed.

Neurolinguistic Programming is an excellent mode that can clarify the way people comprehend and communicate. To capsulize the premise of Neurolinguistic Programming, there are three basic ways that people process information. Each individual has a special way of learning, comprehending, and communicating. One person might be auditory, another visual, and another kinesthetic. If a person comprehends through hearing, better communication can be facilitated by using the words "I hear" in sentences. If, however, a person is visual and learns through seeing, the buzz words, "I see" stimulate his comprehension. Another person may sense things, or feel them. In this instance, communications need to relate to feelings. The words "I feel" help get a message across.

A simple test of eye movement is a method of determining which category an individual may fit into. A person may have more than one way of comprehending, and therefore will fall into additional categories when the testing is done on a comprehensive level. If basic problems exist in the way two people communicate with each other, those conflicts exist from the very beginning of a relationship. Even though these two people may love each other deeply, if they cannot talk to each other, misunderstandings grow into mountain-size barriers to love.

Astrology can offer an even deeper understanding of the way people communicate and interact with each other. By comparing two horoscopes, it is very easy to determine basic compatibility that can exist from the very beginning of a relationship. Early patterns become very clear, to a practiced astrologer, just by looking at the placement of the planets in the wheel of the chart. The conditions that surround a person in childhood, especially in connection with the kind of affection from parents and family members, have a great deal to do with the way an individual expresses love and affection later on. An astrological chart is particularly helpful in describing what we look for in a partnership situation, and can pinpoint the characteristics that we actually attract in a partner. As an example, a person may want personal freedom in a relationship and may attract someone who is unpredictable. The personal freedom is assured, but in a nonproductive way. If the same person is aware from the beginning of a relationship just what it is that he or she really wants, he or she can recognize the quality in another person. With advance knowledge, the person can find someone who encourages freedom to exist in a relationship, but who is also reliable and considerate.

Most often we are attracted to another person who actually has the specific qualities we need for balance in our lives, but those qualities are not what we would design for ourselves from a personality level. We most often get what we want, without realizing what it was that we really asked for in a relationship. An astrological chart can accurately describe those subtle, underlying patterns and can be an essential tool for marriage counseling, as an example.

Even more important might be the practice of consulting an astrologer before the bonds between two people have already been established. There must be give and take in a relationship, but it is easier to adjust to another person when we know exactly what we must adjust to. Life patterns that have already been developed in relation to love, communications, emotional reactions, and special interests can easily determine the level of compatibility between people. The placement of the planets in a natal horoscope describes the way those qualities are expressed and released in life. When astrology is used as a tool for the determination of compatibility, a particular number of planets need to be located at the same degrees in two charts. Even if the placement of those connecting planets are not always in harmonious signs, the chances of two people growing together are very strong. A little bit of friction can be important in a relationship, or the partnership might become deadly dull. However, the friction must stimulate growth and excitement, or the relationship could eventually be very detrimental. The conflict might easily cause nastiness and abusive behavior to build up in a relationship. It often happens that two people are bonded together in a relationship where very few planets match up according to degree and sign. This situation might indicate that two people live in close proximity to each other, but lead completely separate lives. The lack of connection, indicated by a chart, can often happen in a marriage where sexual attraction is mistaken for long-lasting love, or love blinds two people to a lack of harmony physically, mentally, and emotionally. Boredom and disinterest lead to apathy, in such a situation, but fortunately, the relationship would be devoid of violence.

Eventually, and hopefully, astrology will become even more accepted as a valuable tool for understanding the deeper underlying structure of life.

Businesses could benefit tremendously by having a staff astrologer in a personnel office. A great deal of time and money could be saved by taking a short amount of time to see whether or not a person will fit into an already existing group of people working together. Even a brilliant and accomplished person can do very little in a corporate structure if he or she has personality clashes with coworkers and is butting heads with everyone around him.

An astrological chart can quite clearly show that opposites attract. There is no more powerful pull of attraction than the magnetic appeal of oppositions. In the beginning of an association, opposing qualities are intriguing. If love is strong and mutual respect is deep, two people on opposite ends of the seesaw learn from each other. As partners begin to mirror each other, there is binding strength in the balance that can be achieved by recognizing the value of opposite qualities.

More often than not, however, each person may begin to say, "Why aren't you more like me?" As recognition of a lack within each person is reflected by another, each partner can begin to resent the very qualities that attracted them in the first place. Relationships can become quite boring if there is no friction between two people. That friction must obviously exist in ways that are stimulating, not hurtful. As the world approaches the true dawning of the Age of Aquarius, the system of astrological analysis is becoming more popular. Many people have gone past the basics of knowing their own birth sign and are beginning to use computer programs to set up their own charts.

The problem with using any of these wonderful systems of analysis—color typing, Myers-Briggs testing, NLP or astrology—is that the systems can only pinpoint areas of stress in relationships. The systems themselves cannot heal and resolve anything. Mankind can take a giant step forward in developing levels of tolerance and understanding by using these systems, but when a crisis occurs, the mere understanding of what might be occurring won't solve the problem. The developed technique of response that comes from comprehension of the patterns can often fly away at the very moment they are needed most.

The benefits of a regression session are different from mere analysis, as resultant awareness goes deeply into the psyche. A true healing occurs when information comes forth about a relationship that may have existed in a past life. Usually that information is so astounding that it automatically changes a perspective about what appears to be the present-day patterns. The revealed information not only explains another person's behavior or actions but, more importantly, reveals **why** we react in a particular way. We cannot change the behavior of someone else, but when we change our own perspective, the natural reaction is automatically different.

In the light of reincarnation we repeat the same patterns over and over, and over again. If we have loved someone deeply and well in a past existence, that love spills over into the present time. If we have disliked someone, or taken action against an individual, we seem drawn back like a magnet to review the situation and get it right at last.

Reincarnation is just like yesterday to today. If we had a fight or argument with someone during the daytime, and go to sleep hurt or angry, we awaken to a new day with the same feelings. Invariably, any attraction has its roots in a previous existence. It is unlikely that we meet people with whom we have a strong association unless we have some kind of past connection. Recognition of another person that we have known in the past usually happens almost instantaneously. From the viewpoint of reincarnation, any sense of harmony or degree of comfort that is prevalent in a relationship indicates a past-life tie. And if we have instant dislike or feel repelled, there is usually a logical reason for that feeling as well. If we have no past association with an individual, the person probably feels like a stranger. Marriage counselors advise couples never to go to sleep angry. That is a good habit to develop in any situation, and is wise advice, for if we resolve a problem before sleep (or before death), we come back with less stress and disharmony in our lives.

We can change our relationships with others by simply acknowledging what went wrong and finding a solution. Often the solution is as simple as saying "I'm sorry." It is usually more difficult to forgive ourselves, or to accept that we may have been wrong. But as sure as day follows night, any separation must be resolved before we are able to progress on our own evolutionary path. To realize that we might have to go through the same pattern with the same person lifetime after lifetime is encouragement enough to get it right in present time.

We do not always come together, in the present existence, with people who have been loving and kind in a past life. If we have loved wisely and well, we awaken to those same warm feelings. More often than not, as might be indicated by the current high divorce rate and family problems, we are attracted to karmic relationships where past lives were very conflicted. If this is the case, it can be very important to take a look at the past to heal a current relationship through awareness, compassion, and forgiveness. In the process of resolving karmic knots, however, we do not have to suffer at the hands of another. For that is not taking care of oneself. Since we are all one, any sin against oneself is a sin against all others.

Ideally, both parties involved in an antagonistic relationship might go through an individual regression session. Each person can then review his or her particular viewpoint from the past and identify the patterns in the present. A discussion after such an exercise can be tremendously enlightening. But it is quite amazing that even if only one partner goes to a past life, the new perspective gleaned by that person can seem to help the other person as if they were talking through the airwaves. The situation can begin to be healed through any level of new comprehension and discussion, even nonverbal, for it is true . . . thoughts are things.

HEALING A MOTHER-DAUGHTER RELATIONSHIP

Dorothy was especially cool and unyielding to her mother's overtures of friendship, even from early childhood. No obvious problem existed between the two women, such as anger and fighting, but there was a distinct lack of closeness. Dorothy booked an appointment with me, unaware that she would focus on her relationship with her mother. Throughout her regression session Dorothy said, "I know she loves me, but I won't allow myself to respond to her." Clara, the mother, was extremely hurt by this. Dorothy said, "My mother's friends chastise me by saying, 'Your mother is a wonderful person. You're really hurting her a lot by your behavior. Can't you just try to be nice to her?' "

Dorothy's regression session shocked her into an awareness of the depth of her love for her mother. Dorothy discovered that she actually felt fear of intimacy with her mother as a result of unconscious guilt. When Dorothy went back to her past life, she saw herself as a young mother, married to a nice man she loved, and living in a cold-water flat in New York City. She saw herself giving her adored baby a bath. As she turned away for a few seconds to get a towel, the baby slipped under the water and drowned.

The young mother never recovered from her loss. She felt tremendous guilt over her baby's death. Dorothy was shocked to realize that the baby was her mother in the present life.

Some months later, Dorothy called to tell me some astounding news. Her mother was forced to remain in bed after back surgery. Dorothy said, "I really wanted to go live with my mother during her recuperation. I even gave up my vacation so that I could take care of her. We're very close now, and I'm so happy! My mother's friends cannot imagine what happened to make such a difference in my attitude. You can imagine how happy I've made my mother and, of course, myself."

Throughout ages we have fought and loved, betrayed and killed, sacrificed and abandoned those we have come in contact with. In the present existence, we come back again to rectify wrongs and restore the balance. We may have been perpetrators, and sometimes victims.

Every association, productive or nonproductive, has its inception in a past life, and it is only in the light of reincarnation that many present-day relationships make sense. The roots of current problems have already been firmly planted. What we are dealing with are only the flowers or weeds that show aboveground. Healing can take place when we find, and dig up, the root of the problems.

Resolving troubled relationships while we are still on earth not only enables us to bring more joy and happiness into the present existence, but it is key for the programming of a future life. The patterns of the past repeat themselves very accurately. If we accidentally hit our head on a beam and wound ourselves, the wound is still evident when we awaken the next day. So it is true with all patterns from life to life. If we have had an argument with someone, or have been hurt, the decisions made at that moment are still in our consciousness as we enter a new life.

People in troubled relationships (and that includes almost everyone) are searching for ways to release pressure and find solutions. If we take a look at the high divorce rate and the large number of people searching for guidance with therapists, psychics, and astrologers, it is not hard to imagine how any book that might shed light on past life associations can help the public at large. Magazine articles about regression sessions are fanning their readers' desire to find answers to present problems by searching the past.

Hopefully this book will help to clarify, augment, expand, and heal present-day difficulties by shedding light on some common problems. The most important test that comes with earthly existence has to do with healing these interpersonal interactions. Until we identify, and "love" our brothers and sisters, we cannot reach true enlightenment. Ultimately, we are all *one*. A crime against our fellow man is a crime against the self. The opposite is also true.

We pick up, in the present, exactly where we left off at death in the past. If we have developed a high level of consciousness and awareness before death, we continue to exist on that plane in the "in-between" state, or on the spiritual planes. If we have persisted in spiritual blindness, and remain asleep in life, we awaken in that same state. We may have a new personality, new physical characteristics, and different relationships, but the knots on the thread of consciousness that weave through our lifetimes are still there. The beautiful golden stitches are there, too. All we have to do is reclaim them in the present.

The purpose of conducting a regression session without the use of hypnosis is to teach the individual how to dialogue with his own subconscious in a conscious, wide-awake state. When he or she learns to access information on his own, he or she continues to gain additional insights almost automatically, especially if a problem arises that seems to defy logical explanation. This can be especially beneficial in resolving difficult relationships.

CHAPTER 2

Regression therapy; how it heals problematic relationships in the present.

According to the theory of reincarnation, life follows life just as each day follows the previous one. Lifetime to lifetime is like yesterday to today. Death is like sleep between days and rebirth like getting up and putting on a new body or suit of clothes. The memories that linger like a continuous thread continue to haunt long after the event is forgotten. Reactions to people we love or hate and behavior characteristics can stem from seemingly unimportant events that were never resolved in a past life. Very real-life problems, physical disabilities, and psychological blocks can usually be explained by a past life traumatic situation that lies at the core of the matter.

Shakespeare said, "All the world's a stage, And all the men and women merely players." According to metaphysical principles, life is indeed a drama of our creation. Carl Jung said, "Any unrealized energy or potential exteriorizes as fate or destiny." All that might be interpreted to mean that we consciously, or unconsciously, set in motion the specific circumstances and conditions around us. Theoretically, then, we are not victims of our environment but rather the creators of it. If that is so, why are we not all successful, healthy, happy, and constantly on top of any situation? Who would deliberately pick illness, physical disability, poverty, isolation, loneliness, or despair? Yet all we have to do is look around to see heartrending difficulties in people's lives, especially in relationships.

The attempt to understand the human condition is not a new one. For centuries, philosophical man has explored the workings of the human mind, taking a variety of approaches to delving within the subconscious, hoping to find the key to more successful living. Descartes decided that existence was directly related to thought processes when he said, "I think, therefore I am." Carl Jung went giant steps farther and described what he termed the collective unconscious. His theory was that man not only had his own subconscious memories but could also tap a universal memory bank that contained the genetic codes and thought forms of mankind as a whole. It is by tapping this level of consciousness that we can uncover personal memory of past lives. The memories of life spent on another stage can explain these karmic attractions, relationships, and sexual leanings. Physical health, talent, and intellect, among other things, are qualities that, like pearls on a string, follow us from lifetime to lifetime. Memories of traumas, shock, and loss are like knots on the thread of consciousness.

There is an interplay of characters from lifetime to lifetime. Ruth Montgomery says in her book *The*

World Before, "Human beings, like Cervantes' birds of a feather who flock together, tend to reincarnate in cycles with those they have known in previous earthly sojourns. By some curious law of karmic attraction we return again and again with these perennial companions to work out mutual problems left unresolved, or enjoy each other's company."

How can we integrate information from past-life memories into present time? Can the details we release into consciousness really help solve new problems that continue to arise as soon as one set of difficulties seems resolved? If we are really creating the circumstances of our daily-life scripts, where does religion enter in, and who is the real mastermind of our drama? Why do we still have conflicts and personality clashes if we become more aware of action and interaction, cause and effect? Do we always act as a mirror for the people we encounter in relationships? Where did it all begin?

The roots of these patterns go very deep into the subconscious, like the submarine depths of an iceberg. These patterns may lie at the very beginning of time itself, when mankind first began to cut away from the one force or God consciousness. Edgar Cayce, sometimes called "The Sleeping Prophet," explained creation by describing it this way. He said the original feeling of comfort and security in the oneness of existence, on a spiritual plane, gave way to a need for individuation. The soul desire for expansion of consciousness led to a search for new experiences. Sparks of the pure spiritual consciousness began to search for new experiences and, as a result of hovering too close to animal bodies, became trapped on the earth plane. Then came a need for a better physical form for the spirit so that the process of reclaiming the oneness could begin again. With the soul as a dividing line between man and animal, God gave mankind the gift of free will. So it is free will that enables man to evolve back to the sublime, again at his own rate of speed. It may take centuries of missing that divine comfort and perfect harmony for the spirit to reach the highest state again. In a regression session, one young woman I worked with described the sensation of being in between lives by saying, "I'm like a squiggly in a sea of bliss, but I have no sense of individuality. So I have to incarnate to feel my own boundaries again."

Eventually Edgar Cayce, a man steeped in traditional religious beliefs, came to accept the theory of reincarnation as truth, but only when it was clear that the material he was revealing had a positive effect on the lives of his subjects. It was stressed in his readings that a practical approach to the idea of many lives was very necessary. Memories of a previous existence were unimportant and could even be detrimental unless the individual applied that knowledge to present-life conditions. On no account were these memories to be used as an ego builder or a rationale for conduct. To let the glamour of a memory of a previous high position, for instance, obscure the lesson that was to be learned in the present life could actually delay spiritual growth.

To take one life memory away from the whole cloth might also obscure the overall picture, for indeed the thread running from life to life could have woven around it a gamut of experiences. Lives could run from high to low, exciting to routine, productive to static, as was required for soul development. The central theme running through all those levels of existence might indicate that present-day circumstances are not so very different from past-life conditions, no matter what the outer trappings. It seems we take centuries upon centuries to learn some lessons. In her book *Many Lives, Many Loves,* Gina Cerminara clearly states, "It is significant, I think, that the theory of reincarnation and karma is one of uncompromising accountability and responsibility."

From this perspective, the concept of original sin is quite different from that held by traditional religion. The word "sin" in Spanish means "without." In the approaching Aquarian Age, the separation of man from the God force within (man without soul consciousness) is the real sin. It is ultimately the soul that is the connecting link between God and mankind on the highest level. After enough struggles on the earth plane, or in the school of life, man begins to long for that divine connection again. It may be that the struggles on earth are connected to one's sorrow and inability to forgive oneself for breaking the all-important connection in the first place.

Subjects of regression sessions have seen themselves as kings and commoners, beggars and thieves, saints and sages. But invariably, a deep sense of relief comes with released memories, no matter what kind of experience is uncovered from the past. The process of recollection seems to automatically resolve a range of issues. Little by little, the experience of past-life memory begins to be integrated into present-day existence quite naturally. An individual becomes aware of having a different perspective about a particular situation or relationship almost immediately, and that seems to heal the present conditions.

Sometimes another person in a troubled relationship may be unaware of the session and the information that has come forth, but can also be healed. A dramatic example of that kind of healing took place when Eileen called to book a regression session with me over the telephone. She had already told me that she thought she might have lived during World War II, and she thought she might have been a child being chased by dogs. Her nightmares had been very disturbing. She was also very unsure about her pending engagement to a man who said he loved her deeply. But Eileen didn't know if she could believe that his love for her was real. She was also very upset over her relationship with her brother in the present time. Rather than directly focusing on the issues she had in mind, and after reviewing her childhood, I directed Eileen to go to a past life that would give an explanation to her present-day situation. Eileen said, "Oh, here we go. This is the one I've been waiting for. Oh, my God." Eileen burst into tears and said, "It's the dream I had in mind, but I'm not the one getting chased, I'm the one holding the dogs! Oh, my God."

After a moment of silence, I asked if she had been male or female and how old she was. She replied, "I'm a man, and I'm in my twenties. I'm German, and I'm the one holding a dog." Through her tears she said, "It's a German shepherd, and I'm chasing kids. I thought it was me, but it is the other way around." I gave Eileen as much comfort as possible, and assured her that she would experience a healing if she could just look more closely at the circumstances.

Eileen continued, "I'm with other soldiers, and we're in the country. I see a dirt road and an old farmhouse. I'm in uniform, and I'm holding one of two dogs. There are people running in every direction. Someone finds three or four children and chases them out of the barn." She paused for a moment, and I could hear a fresh bunch of tears as she said, "I'm just a child myself. I'm among the group of soldiers who are supposed to find people in hiding. We are going from the city through a small town to another destination, but we see this farmhouse and stop. The family that is hiding these children is not Jewish.

"The dogs are barking like crazy. They're making a great deal of noise. My dog starts barking, but I hold on to him with all my strength. He's pulling me, trying to chase the running children. The children are so scared and are running as fast as they can, but of course we catch them. The family is inside the farmhouse, and they don't come out. The person in charge opens the door to the barn and finds the children in the hay. One of them is a little boy just about three years old." After a moment, when fresh tears emerged, Eileen said, "I didn't think I'd have to do something like this. I'm just drafted and have to go into the army. I really don't want to do this job, but I'm a soldier and have to obey orders. All the children are captured except for one of them who gets away." Eileen gasped as she said, "Oh, I let him get away. There is so much confusion. I'm supposed to be chasing this boy. He appears to be about twelve years old. I hold on to my dog until he can run off into the woods, and he runs really fast."

There was a moment of silence before I asked Eileen what happened when the other soldiers discovered that one child had escaped. She thought for a moment and said, "Well, I'm back in the car, and there is an explosion. Oh, I don't belive this! We're back in the Jeep, and I'm shot in the back by my friend. I can't believe my fellow soldiers would do this." I asked Eileen if she knew that soldier in this life. She replied, "I think that person is my brother in this life." Eileen had already described an extremely difficult relationship with her sibling in this lifetime. He stayed away from her as much as possible and refused to share family responsibilities with her when crisis times arose. Eileen said, "That would explain a lot of things." I asked Eileen how this brother would feel, on a soul-consciousness level, about shooting her in the back. She replied, "No wonder he doesn't want to have anything to do with me." Eileen suddenly took a deep breath and said, "I think the boy who got away is my fiancé." I said, "He must love you so much." She said, "I think he does." I commented on how fortunate she is to find someone who will be very loyal and loving to her.

I spoke to Eileen the following morning to make sure she was feeling comfortable about our session. After telling me she was fine, she said, "It surely has given me a lot to think about. By the way, I spoke to my fiancé last night. I didn't tell him I was doing a regression session, but as he was saying good-bye, he told me he loved me. That is absolutely not something he would ordinarily say over the phone. I was really surprised." The spontaneous expression of his love for Eileen was obviously stimulated by her memory of the sacrifice she had made for him in Germany during World War II. Eileen is now married to the man she saved, and they have a new baby. Eileen is ecstatically happy. The power of the mind is formidable. With a new perspective, we make new decisions almost automatically and begin to rewrite our life script.

It is important to resolve troubled relationships while we are still on earth. That effort to restore harmony is not only essential for more joy and happiness in our present existence, but it is also the key for the programming of a future life. If an understanding can be gained about present-day relationships, and information can be reached about what might have happened between two people in a past go 'round, some of these knots give way, but first there is another ingredient that must take place.

The ability to forgive is the most important part of a review of past lives. If one can resolve conflicts before departing from the earth plane, a future life can be free from those restrictive patterns of hatred, anger, and vindictiveness. When the mandate to forgive is recognized from a reincarnation point of view, it becomes less of a "Pollyanna," altruistic concept of "Love your enemies" and becomes the most important ingredient for the rest of one's own future well-being because every act has a reaction or boomerang effect.

Guilt appears to be a hook that keeps us coming back to nonproductive situations over and over again. If we could wave our magic wand and walk past our karma, why don't we do so? It is a deep sense of guilt that prevents us from the freedom of joyous choices and activity in our lives. Another problem that prevents that joy lies in the exactitude of balance from life to life. If we consider how many small injustices we allow to go by on a daily basis, it is no wonder that it takes thousands of lifetimes to set the record straight, for in the light of reincarnation, no one gets away with anything! Every small thing must be balanced and reconciled. The slate must be wiped clean. Imagine: Every thought or deed against another human being must be resolved. No wonder mankind is still struggling to come into the light of new conditions. Acknowledging responsibility for past actions is a first step to take, but we must know what that responsibility really means. Self-forgiveness may be the next step to take.

In between each lifetime the soul has a chance to rest on another level of consciousness just as between each day we have a chance to sleep. Nighttime gives the physical body a rest and an opportunity to recuperate, but another important function can also take place. The subconscious mind can reveal important information through dreams when the conscious mind is temporarily at rest. Dreams are a way of tapping into knowledge that might otherwise remain hidden.

Some people are aware of their dreams and take advantage of that extra insight, and some people hardly know they dream at all. Death, like sleep, gives the physical body a chance to renew itself. It is also the time to review the circumstances and events of the previous existence in order to set in motion the conditions for a new life, like going through a checklist to see what needs to be repaired. However, just like the dreams we may not remember, many people are not yet aware that tapping into past lives can reveal amazing information, bringing new insights and significance to our daily existence. Just as we tend to forget, or ignore, the events of a previous day, most people forget the events of a previous life. Sometimes that is a blessing, unless we are ready and prepared to deal with information that may demand a new level of responsibility.

The attempt to remember dreams can be accomplished in several ways. Some people keep a pad and pencil by the bedside to write down their dreams in the middle of the night or keep a tape recorder under the pillow. When nightly dreams are interpreted and transcribed into a journal, the results can be like a fascinating road map of daily insights. Hopefully psychological and spiritual growth is the result of such efforts. Dreams give clarity to the workings of the inner self and enrich daily existence with endlessly fascinating wonders that one might never be able to conceive through imagination alone. In one instance, the analysis of a young woman's horrifying recurring nightmare led to her own revelation of a lifetime as a victim in a concentration camp during World War II. Eve was able to give me exact details of that life as she sat opposite me with her eyes wide open. Her dreams had been her subconscious message to herself to bring many horrifying memories into daylight again so they could be resolved and would never haunt her in her new life. Eve discovered that no matter what she suffered as a victim, at the bottom of her pain there was a key issue demanding self-forgiveness.

A regression session can be like a trip we might take through a foreign country. We see infinite delights that appeal to our senses, giving richer experiences to take home with us again. We find that we begin to adopt some customs or habits learned on our trip. We might begin to enjoy taking time out for afternoon tea, as an example, after a trip to England. The reclaiming of former creative abilities can be one distinct advantage of reviewing past lives. After a regression session, forgotten facets of creativity begin to automatically merge into present consciousness.

Imagine tapping into information about a previous existence in such a way that thoughts and visions, customs and habits continue to pop into consciousness almost anytime at all. Once an individual has learned how to dialogue with his own subconscious, the doors are open for all kinds of new experiences. Information that is revealed in this way can bring at the very least, endlessly fascinating metaphors that help incorporate new conditions into present-life patterns. It is not even necessary to believe in reincarnation for such miracles to occur. It is truly amazing to see how we might cast a present-life loved one, or a villain, in a new role at a different time in history, as if we were writing a novel or a film script. It is truly spectacular to have a vision of a different era float into consciousness and to realize that we are either geniuses at writing a subtext to give meaning to present-day conditions, or else the mind has a fascinating way of re-creating exact scenarios in the present time that reflect the past.

In a regression session, those experiences, memories, or fantasies emerge backward, as it were. Imagine photographing an automobile involved in an explosion. When the film is run backward, all the pieces of that car fly through the air from the wrong direction, floating into place easily to produce the original outline of the automobile in its entirety. So it is with a regression session. The story emerges line by line, scene by scene, but in reverse order, only to be connected to experiences in this life after the session is complete.

The conscious mind seems to allow specific memories to come forth only when we are ready for them.

Other details may emerge over a period of time when we least expect them, but the resulting feeling of released emotion indicates that those memories are meaningful and very potent, even years after the original regression session. The incredible wealth of storytelling that lurks in the mind of almost everyone is astounding.

I vividly recall a session with a man who lived in an industrial area. He was retired, after having worked very hard all his life. He was of a practical nature and might not be expected to be interested in exploring what might be only a fantasy. However, the pictures emerged very easily. He saw himself at age two, dressed in a white dress, as was the custom in his youth. But he was quite surprised to discover that he could actually see the texture of the lace used to decorate that dress, worn many years before and never consciously recalled earlier in his life. He then saw himself at about eight months, expressing curiosity about a can of paint. He knew he was wearing only diapers, and knew that the color of the paint was green. He knew the exact shade of green and felt himself putting that delicious color all over his body. He also felt the pain of being cleaned up. He was stripped of his diapers, put in a tub, and liberally soaked with turpentine to remove the paint from his body. His screams still rang in his ears. This man had no problem accepting the reality of that experience in his babyhood, even though the incident had never been discussed before. He readily accepted the experiences that poured forth about his past lives. No matter how much time elapses, the exact details and memories do not fade.

These experiences usually come forth from the subconscious with accompanying deep emotion. If indeed the person is not living a real moment from his past, he is a genius of an actor as well as a writer. He never knows the final outcome of the plot until he reaches the dropped stitch of his trauma. Many times the subject of such a session asks, "Do you think I made that up?" My reply is, "What do you think?" He or she usually says, after a moment's pause, "I couldn't have. It was just so real."

Life between life can be a sort of schoolroom where the soul can evaluate the mistakes on earth. Like summer school, where events of the school year can be reviewed and decisions made about the experiences to be undertaken in the new semester, a soul can prepare for the next karmic go-round. However, the soul must return to earth and be in a physical body, in order to reconcile events and balance the scales of past mistakes. Therefore, it is much easier to heal the wounds in the present existence rather than having to suffer another whole life trying to resolve problems that have accumulated over many lifetimes. That would be like having to repeat grades in school over, and over, again.

If an understanding can be reached about what might have happened between two people and forgiveness can take place, the situation is then completely healed. After such an experience, we can truly begin to enrich the lives of those we touch through our own newfound joyfulness. If we clean a dusty window, the sunlight can begin to shine through.

MEANING OF KARMA

The word *karma* simply means "the law." It is the term that describes the biblical phrase, An eye for an eye, a tooth for a tooth. We all know that in one lifetime, this ancient law simply doesn't work. People get away with many actions, even murder, without any obvious punishment.

In the book *Ponder on This*, based on the writings of Alice Bailey and the Tibetan Master Dhwal Khul, a discussion of karma reveals, "The law of karma is the most stupendous law of the system and one which is impossible for the average man in any way to comprehend, for, if traced back along its central root and its many ramifications, one eventually reaches the position where causes antedating the solar system have to be dealt with. . . . This law really concerns, or is based on causes which are inherent in the constitution of matter itself and on the interaction between atomic units, whether we use this expression in connection with an atom of substance, a human being, a planetary atom, or a solar atom."

However profound and true is that statement, we can only deal with the simplest analysis of the effect of karmic law on one person's life . . . that is, our own. In doing so, it is important to stress the positive as well as the negative concept of karma. It seems we focus on the continual retribution, that is part of this concept, and punish ourselves unmercifully, aeons into aeons. This is somewhat like trying to dig the golf ball out of the sand trap with an inappropriate club. The ball goes deeper and deeper. But it is possible to forfeit points and start again with a new ball. In life, we seem to overlook the possibility of quickly reviewing our karmic debts in order to relieve ourselves of burdens. It is more common to continue to hack away nonproductively with the wrong club, lifetime after lifetime.

Outer circumstances may teach us many lessons, but true awareness comes from an inner search. It is not hard to imagine how a regression session can fan the flame of curiosity about our own individual history. New information can only whet a desire to find all the answers to present-day problems through searching out our past. Like discovering information about our ancestors through genealogical charts, it is even more astounding to uncover our genealogical history throughout many, many lives. It is often the case that in our search, we discover a tie-in with present-life names, locations, and special interests we've already had in connection to particular cultures.

REGRESSION WITHOUT HYPNOSIS

It is possible to tap memories or concepts of past-life experiences without the use of drugs, hypnosis, or any other artificial means. We have easier access

to our unconscious than we may imagine. After
thousands of regression sessions conducted with the
subject's mind fully open, conscious and aware,
there have been only two or three people who were
unable to get to an important past-life memory. The
information that is within the human mind is stag-
gering. A person undergoing the session experiences
a new part of his inner being for the first time. Even
after years of psychoanalysis, one subject expressed
amazement that she had touched on matters that
had never been hinted at in her sessions of analysis.

No matter what technique is utilized to regress
people to past lives, most practitioners agree on the
purpose and benefits of a regression session. That
purpose is not for titillation of the ego, but to clarify
and bring forth the fears, restrictions, guilts, and
sometimes malicious events of the past in order to
make more appropriate choices in the here and now.

As an example, one situation that becomes crys-
talline with a new perspective is a rather common
feeling of loneliness in the present time. There are
several reasons why such a feeling exists. There have
been many cases in which a person saw no other
way out of the loneliness and sense of frustration
than to commit suicide in a past life. The result is a
new life with even more intense feelings of loneliness because not only was there self-harm, but there
is the added karma of depriving others of our love,
companionship, and association. The individuals
who have chosen suicide as their way out in past
lives are not released from the confines of the earth

plane until the natural time of death. It is my understanding that they must wander, trapped, on the
earth plane without the protective shield of a body.
That would be like deliberately driving an automobile over a cliff and then having to walk everywhere without the benefit of a car, for no good
reason at all. Better to have the use of an automobile,
which can facilitate getting around, to solve the current problems. Even the most successful, dynamic,
and intelligent people have cycles and patterns that
can turn their lives around at a moment's notice. Op-
timism then falls desperately short of effectiveness
in the face of suicides, death, or tragic accidents.
Modern therapy seems to have found some answers,
yet the road to fulfillment can seem like a long one.
Attempts to change lifelong habits and patterns can
seem like a slow and painstaking trip to the top of
Mount Everest. But even in the depths of despair,
there is always one more step to take. Can a regression session really be a surefire way to achieve a different perspective? Is past-life information the magic
answer to it all?

An important part of a regression process is to
learn to trust the ability to have a dialogue between
the conscious and unconscious mind. This trust can
be established by first learning how to ask the right
kinds of questions and then to be willing to accept
the answers that come to mind. It is necessary to put
the skeptical part of the mind aside and allow oneself to listen to the answer within. It is not necessary
to believe in reincarnation to tap these memories, for

whether these memories are real or fancied does not really matter. If they emerge from within, they belong to us and clearly give an explanation to present-day problems or circumstances. The willingness to avoid making judgments about whether those answers are correct seems the only prerequisite to a successful regression session.

Each individual already has the answers to queries in his own subconscious mind. The theory is that an answer is inherent in the question. In our society it is fairly common to ask opinions of other people rather than taking responsibility to trust ourselves to come up with solutions. An ideal to work toward is the inner communication that can come as a result of inner dialogues. Trust may have to be carefully nurtured before the subconscious will open up a stream of information. The questions a person asks himself are directed toward the higher, intuitive mind, going beyond the concrete mind, and the questions must be asked with a real intention of getting an answer.

So the real purpose of conducting a regression session without the use of hypnosis is to teach the individual how to dialogue with his own subconscious in a conscious, wide-awake state. When he or she learns to ask the right questions in the process of accessing information, he or she continues in that ability, gaining additional insights almost automatically. This can be especially helpful if a later problem arises that seems to defy logical explanation. A person can ask inner questions and get right answers because each individual already has all the answers within. The ability to go through this process is especially beneficial in resolving difficult relationships.

It may take years of traditional therapy to resolve a situation where a person is stuck in a relationship. Ultimately, the individual may not accomplish much more than learning how to cope with a seemingly impossible situation, or becoming resigned to unhappiness in life. We cannot divorce parents, children, and siblings, and oftentimes we cannot divorce a marital partner, either. It can seem difficult to walk away from an unloving, but committed, liaison at times. A regression session can explain why this may be so difficult.

In the process of going back to a past life, a person asks a question of his higher mind, and then listens to the answer within. For many people, the hard part is trusting that the impressions which come to mind are valid. Therefore, it is essential to acknowledge mental impressions without trying to prove that they are real. Sometimes an individual can actually see pictures that form within the mind's eye. Sometimes a person only gets a "sense" of something. Even if an individual feels those pictures or sensations are only fantasy, they belong to the person searching for the answer. They come from within the mind, not from an external source; therefore they have validity.

One of the most important opportunities offered by a regression session is the ability to review events while still on earth, thereby speeding up soul evolution. It is usually necessary to return to earth and be in a physical body, in order to reconcile events and balance the scales of past mistakes. Therefore, it is much easier to heal the wounds in the present existence rather than having to suffer another whole life trying to resolve problems that have accumulated over many lifetimes.

I have a strong feeling about doing a regression session without hypnosis. I am concerned about the possibility of putting something into the subconscious mind through hypnosis that is inaccurate or simply didn't exist for the individual prior to the session. When a person is fully conscious, awake, and aware, he sees everything from the perspective of the here and now. He sees time in a different way and learns how to have a dialogue with his own inner mind. The procedure activates a part of the thinking process that may have been dormant before and reveals an ability to pull forth answers from within that the subject may not have known were available to him.

Wilhelm Reich's theory that all memories of pain or trauma are encapsulated in the muscular structure certainly can apply to past lives. In a moment of pressure, worry, or fear, we tend to tense some part of the body to hold on for survival. We can therefore release a lot of energy and restore abundant health by knowing where that tension resides in the body and how it began. The process of going back to a past life can eliminate a lot of hard mental work in the present. Awareness enables a release to occur physically, mentally, and emotionally. The reactions are spontaneous and continue to have benefit long after the session is over. Until we identify and "love" our brothers, we cannot reach true enlightenment. Forgiveness of self and others is the key to unlocking the door to future happiness.

CHAPTER 3

Eternal love;
back together again.

Since the word "karma" has become somewhat familiar to many people, we tend to equate that with negative situations in our lives. There is at least a rudimentary understanding of the law of karma: an eye for an eye and a tooth for a tooth. Therefore the usual reaction to the thought of paying off our karmic debts is one of foreboding and dread. However, there is a positive side to karma as well.

No good deed goes unpunished, in the light of the here and now. Transactional Analysis describes a rescue situation that is a hard-and-fast law of interaction between people. In other words, if a rescuer rescues a victim, the victim, in turn, becomes a persecutor, and persecutes the rescuer. The logic behind that axiom is that no one wants to be shown up as inadequate. We are all wherever we are on the scale of evolution because of our individual levels of consciousness. Transactional Analysis also describes another axiom. It is "I'm okay, you're okay." When one person rescues another he is saying, in effect, "I'm okay, you're not okay!"

That leaves mankind in a bit of a dilemma. Are we

not supposed to give a helping hand to those who are less fortunate than we are? Should we ignore the plight of those in need? How can we help people who cannot help themselves? How can we help people retain their sense of dignity when they are incapacitated? An ideal is to help people help themselves, and to have some small exchange of energies going back and forth between the parties involved.

In the light of reincarnation, every deed is rewarded. Every thing we do for another human being, or for animals and the earth is like putting money in a savings account. Sometimes intentions, thoughts, and motivation are enough to create good karma. A classic example of good deeds in the past came from Geoffrey, who realized he had been part of the army headed by Alexander the Great. After a long period of conquest, when Alexander's armies could hardly carry all the appropriated goods, Geoffrey realized that he was fed up over Alexander's gluttony regarding stolen goods. He protested to the men around him about taking more confiscated material objects. Those objects would only have to be transported somewhere else. He encouraged a group of Alexander's favorite officers to side with him. When they approached Alexander with a plan to leave some things behind, he ordered them all to be killed. Even though Geoffrey lost his life, he had just placed a great deal of humanitarian gold in the cosmic bank.

Geoffrey came to see me for a past-life regression

when he was the recipient of the session as a gift from a friend of his. Geoffrey's friend, Brett, had a life-changing experience after his own regression session, and very generously wanted to share the experience with his best friends.

Geoffrey had no background in the theory of reincarnation and, in fact, was not at all prepared for what would happen in our time together. It was a successful session, in spite of Geoffrey's figuratively being thrown into the water and told to swim. He was truly surprised at what emerged from his own subconscious.

When Geoffrey described his present life, it was obvious that he resisted accumulating a lot of worldly possession. Geoffrey had courageously left a very cushy job and started his own company, working out of his own apartment. He eventually merged his business with a friend in another city, and decided to relocate. His company attracted major clients, and Geoffrey was able to establish beautifully decorated offices. He found a nice apartment in a trendy section of that city, but it was clear that the interior decor of his apartment was very different from his offices. In fact, it was fairly typical of a bachelor pad. For example, it was my understanding that Geoffrey kept his bicycle on the wall. He almost had a phobia about accumulating too many worldly goods. At the time he was describing his lifestyle, he had not bothered to question his resistence to a more lavish ambience.

The painful situation that Geoffrey first reviewed

in his present life had to do with a recent traumatic experience with a woman he loved. He had broken off their engagement a very short time before the wedding was to take place. All the gifts had to be returned, and his longtime, live-in relationship ended abruptly.

The situation was not easy. Geoffrey is a very loving, caring, affectionate person. He did not want to hurt Kelly, but he just couldn't bring himself to commit to a marriage. I don't believe Geoffrey understood his own reaction to the situation. He loved Kelly, and there was no doubt about that love being returned, for Geoffrey was the love of Kelly's life. They were very compatible. The breakup didn't make any sense to anyone. When Geoffrey was describing the situation to me, I couldn't help but feel a lot of compassion for the trauma Kelly must have experienced.

When Geoffrey went to a past life, he saw himself in England, living the life of a successful businessman. His description of his lifestyle was certainly different than the one he chose in the present. He described a beautiful city home . . . probably in London . . . and a beautiful wife, Belinda, that he absolutely adored. In fact, his life revolved around this special woman he was fortunate enough to be married to. As often happens when great devotion is evident in a relationship or marriage, the death of one of the parties is devastating to the person left behind. When Geoffrey's beloved wife died of a slow and lingering illness, he was thrust into a pit of despair. He hardly knew what he was doing after that time.

Luckily, Geoffrey had a housekeeper who had lived with them most of her life. She was practically a member of their family, especially because she had no family of her own. She had diligently and lovingly cared for Belinda until her death. After Belinda's death she was almost as devastated as Geoffrey, for she had been a good friend as well as an employer. Naturally, she stayed on to care for Geoffrey as she had in the past.

Eventually Geoffrey came out of his terrible depression and began to relate to the housekeeper as a woman who was now almost the mistress of the house. Finally, he married her. It was a loving marriage with a bond of affection they both shared for the lovely, deceased Belinda. Geoffrey realized, with a start, that Kelly is the housekeeper he married in the London life. He knew that the reluctance to be married was because he was, on a very unconscious level, waiting for Belinda to show up in his life again.

Many months went past, during which time I formed a lasting friendship with Geoffrey. He asked me to do a regression session with Kelly. They had drifted back into a semicomfortable relationship and had never actually parted ways completely. I was very anxious to meet Kelly, as my compassion for what she must have endured was already well established. I considered Geoffrey to be a very special friend in my life, and even thought I sympathized with Kelly, I could never blame Geoffrey for his sudden change of mind. Since I was aware of the underlying pattern, I could have compassion for both of these wonderful people.

Kelly was quite brave in coming to see me, as she may have suspected I was against her relationship with Geoffrey. She had no way of knowing my true feelings. When she reviewed her present life, she went back to a lifetime that she suspected was in England. Kelly described exactly the same scene as had Geoffrey, but from her point of view. She realized that someone she cared for had died, but that she had actually been in love with her employer throughout the whole time she had worked for the family. She recognized the man as Geoffrey, but she could not identify Belinda among her present-day acquaintances, friends, or family.

Geoffrey had not revealed anything at all to Kelly about his impressions. He wanted her to discover the truth of their relationship very objectively. He was quite anxious to know if she would also have the same memory of their past life together. Kelly left our session with a new outlook on her relationship with Geoffrey and knew that she needed to be very patient if she wanted to be with him in this lifetime. It was a photocopy of the past life, except that Geoffrey had no other love in his life in the present time. Neither Geoffrey nor Kelly worried about someone else coming between them. They seemed to belong together in spite of Geoffrey's reluctance to legitimize their relationship.

Kelly and Geoffrey were married in a very simple ceremony; a far cry from what had been scheduled previously. They eventually decided to have a child, and with great excitement Geoffrey called to tell me the news that Kelly was pregnant. He anticipated being an ideal father. Fortunately, his company was so successful, Geoffrey had no need to spend hours at work, away from his family. He could be a strong partner in the upbringing of their child. They were also able to have as much help as they needed in order to devote themselves to the child they were bringing into the world.

The baby was a little girl. Geoffrey told me that when he saw his daughter, it was love at first sight. Geoffrey and I both knew who the little girl was in their past life. It seemed very clear that she is the adored Belinda, returned to be with both Geoffrey and Kelly once more. In retrospect, Geoffrey's past-life experiences . . . the expression of compassion and love . . . has brought him great abundance, success, and happiness in his present life. His concern about the material belongings and welfare of the people Alexander had conquered, even though thwarted in a past life, seemed to be related to his success in all his endeavors in the present. The deep love expressed in the past enables Geoffrey to be with the two women he loves best in the present time. It is clear to everyone who knows the couple and their adorable daughter that both Kelly and Geoffrey love and cherish their daughter and act as equal partners in her upbringing.

PAST-LIFE DEVOTION

Many people have asked me if their spouse, lover, or best friend could sit in on their regression session. I stress the importance of being in a one-to-one situation with the individual undergoing the session. It is hard to have a level of concentration necessary for the success of the session if someone else is in the room. There is an unconscious sharing of energies with a third party that dilutes the potency of the released memories. However, when Edith and Bill scheduled their regression sessions, I didn't hesitate to agree to their being in the room with each other. I already knew the story of their meeting. Edith's father was a minister in a southern town. Edith, her mother, and her sister were always in attendance at church, quite naturally. They obviously knew everyone in the congregation. Edith sang in the choir, and could see anyone who might enter the sanctuary after the service began. One day a young man who was a stranger to the congregation came to church just as the service was about to begin. Edith saw him and knew, at first glance, that he was the man she would marry. Her mother and sister, sitting in the pews, turned around simultaneously when Bill entered the room and said to each other, "There's Edith's future husband." Both Bill and Edith said, "We have been together in every single lifetime." They simultaneously described a Dutch life when all three of us had been friends. Edith and Bill may have had the happiest marriage of anyone I have ever met.

Sadly Bill, who had been a prominent architect, discovered that he had cancer. In spite of twenty-four hours a day of diligent care, giving Bill everything he needed to reverse the growth, he died. Edith had been with him every moment of the time, fighting by his side to rid his system of the invading malignant cells. When Bill died, she knew she had done whatever she could for him. She also knew she would have to undergo a drastic change in her lifestyle, for she would have to work in order to pay for the major expenses that had been incurred.

With great courage and dignity, Edith entered a new phase of her life. Having had such a depth of love and companionship, one might think Edith would be devastated and incapacitated by her loss. But the strength Bill and Edith gave each other throughout centuries has not only sustained Edith, but she knows with surety it is only a matter of a few hundred or so years when she and Bill will be together again on earth. That, in cosmic time, is only a minute or so to wait for something so wonderful to occur again. Edith has no doubt that she and Bill will share whatever experiences are awaiting on the spiritual plane as well. In fact, Bill's spirit is probably with Edith every day of her life, as long as she is still on the earth plane.

CHAPTER 4

Past-life separations; present-day frustrations.

Many people come to see me for a regression session because of unresolved relationships in the present. However, there were two situations, in particular, that seem to explain, satisfy, and relieve anxieties due to difficult choices in present-day relationships. Both ladies were in a similar situation without knowing each other. Both situations seemed to defy any logical resolution of leftover regret and pangs of love still clinging to their heartstrings. On the surface, there were logical reasons for life decisions about partnership, but both ladies were left in a state of confusion because of a conflict between two men in their lives. If it had been possible to simply make a choice between the two men, and feel good about those choices, the ladies would not find themselves in such a dilemma. But it was not so easy to release the pain over the necessary choice of one person over the other. Over a long period of time, a great deal of anguish was still underlying the life of each lady. Each one could not stop thinking about the man they couldn't be with in the present time. Questions lingered in the mind of each lady. Did she make the right choice? Could she have avoided the hurt over the decisions? What could she do to be free of the lingering confusion? What could she have done differently?

The regression sessions of each person brought forth amazing details about a past life in which the two men played a major role. The impact these men made in the past would not simply vanish over time. For the most part, the men were unaware of the significance of their true relationship to each of these ladies. Both women wanted to have closure with their former lovers so that harmony could exist in any future relationships. Since these men had shown up in several past lives, it was more than likely they would be around in future lives as well.

Eve came to me after having her astrological chart interpreted by me. Since we lived in cities some distance apart, her appointment had been conducted on the telephone. The chart had actually been a gift to her from a man we will call Brett, who was an old friend of hers and a client of mine. Brett told me nothing about Eve except that he recently hired her to work in his office, and wanted to give her a chart as a gift. He added that if she wanted to do a regression session, he would include this in the gift to her, as well.

Brett had met Eve when she was still in college. Eve had interned with Brett's company at that time, but she had now graduated from college and law school. Although she was working for a law firm at the time Brett ran into her again, Brett convinced her to join his staff. What Brett neglected to tell me was how he hired Eve in the first place. Brett was on a trip to a southern town when Eve was still in college. He saw her picture in a local newspaper and told his secretary to hire her as an intern without ever meeting her. After the summer's work Eve went back to school, and Brett lost touch with her. By coincidence, Eve, now married, was living in the city where Brett had his office.

The next time I traveled to the city where Brett and Eve lived, she booked a time for an appointment to do a regression session. When she arrived, I couldn't help but notice her exceptionally pretty face, good figure, lovely smile, and bright eyes. Her intelligence and personality made her come alive with sparkling vivacity and energy.

After we had said our hellos, she laughed and said, "I think I was Brett's first wife!" I dismissed this statement immediately, as I happened to know that Brett had recently divorced his second wife and that his former wife was still alive. I thought to myself, "The things that emerge from a regression session are rarely what people expect," so I didn't comment one way or another about her statement. I actually forgot that she had said that until much later.

Eve reviewed her childhood, which had not been traumatic to any extreme degree, and she described meeting Ed, her husband. She said, "It's as if we have known each other forever. I'm so comfortable with Ed. It was logical from the very beginning that I would marry him." Some things emerged in her review that would help clear her conscience as she was not quite the sweet little southern girl her family thought her to be. She was extremely intelligent, diligently went to church every Sunday with her parents, and was polite and nice. But she had more boyfriends than girlfriends, and she understood that jealousy from some of the girls at school was due to her popularity. She was lucky. She had a loving mother and father, horses of her own to ride, and a nice lifestyle.

Eve had entered a few beauty contests and won, hands down. When she was voted college queen, however, the friction this created made her decide that she was through with beauty contests. It wasn't worth the isolation she felt from other girls, who labeled her as stuck-up and unfriendly. No one seemed to see her as she really was. It hurt, but she shrugged it off and decided to focus on intellectual achievements. That was actually a very major decision in her life, for she had two distinct paths in front of her. Although she knew she had made a conscious choice not to model or study acting, thereby denying a certain part of herself that enjoyed the lure of the glamour world, the regression session showed how important that choice had been for her, how strong that decision was, and how it had changed her life. This lawyer was obviously not just another girl with a pretty face.

When she met Ed, their romance took a very traditional course. They fell in love and had a perfectly beautiful marriage ceremony. She said over and over again, "He is everything to me. He is a brother, lover, husband, and best friend. The big problem is that we hardly need anyone else. We don't go out seeking new friends. We're very content just to be together." With his dark good looks, Ed was a complement to Eve in every way. He was the solid citizen, allowing her to be a free soul. Their love for each other was so secure that Ed was never jealous if she went to important social functions with Brett, her boss. Since she was now part of Brett's organization, those social functions were partly for work, but there was also an element of glamour involved that was a lot of fun for her. Ed didn't begrudge her those experiences. In fact, Ed's agreeable nature surprised people. Eve seemed to have a lot of freedom for a woman in a happy marriage. Once again, other people misunderstood. But Ed knew she needed a certain amount of independence, and it was easy for him to go along with it. Ed's job took him away from home on short trips, but neither one of them, both young and exceptionally good-looking, ever worried about infidelity.

Eve had one problem that didn't fully emerge in the regression session. She had recurring nightmares about a menacing Hitler-Satan-like figure from early childhood. She was afraid she must have done something terrible in a past life. It was as though Satan were haunting her in her dreams. But she dismissed this by saying that Ed would simply hold her when it happened and make it go away.

Eve's past-life memory explained her marriage and comfortable relationship to Ed in the present. She saw that in a past life in Egypt they had been married and were part of a religious group that had some unusual conditions attached to the worship. No one grew old in that society. When a person reached a certain age, it was fully expected that he or she would simply end life by a painless method of suicide, knowing that a better existence awaited on the other side. Loved ones on earth were never burdened with care for elderly people, and they could continue their work unencumbered. When it came time for Eve to go, she wasn't sure she wanted to honor the tradition. She balked a bit, not feeling ready to depart the earth plane, but Ed, her husband in that life also, was fully oriented toward the rules, and felt she should respect the custom and do what was expected of her. There didn't seem to be any real reason to die, from Eve's point of view, but she agreed and followed the ritual of ending her life.

After she was gone, Ed was devastated. He was alone, missed her dreadfully and, in retrospect, couldn't see why her death had been necessary at all. He changed his mind about the group doctrine and was a lost soul for the rest of his life. He not only lost Eve, but the security of his religious beliefs.

Then Eve went to another lifetime. This time she saw herself as a very young, single woman living in an area that resembled Greece. She lived in a small city with her mother and father. There were plans for the family to take an exciting trip that seemed to be connected to her father's business. It was similar to a conference of today, and it was to be held in a large city. It would be a change of pace, at least, and promised to bring new adventures into her life. During a large gathering, which may have been political in nature, she met a man who dazzled her. He seemed to be equally enchanted by Eve, and they made plans to see each other soon after that chance meeting. Their love blossomed rapidly, and since the conference would only last a short time, their future plans had to be made quickly. The only hitch was that this man was already married.

He swore his undying love, and to prove he meant to be with her for the rest of his life, he asked her to go to a distant city to wait for him. Eve couldn't go back home now, for she was no longer a virgin and would disgrace her family if she announced she was involved with this man. Evidently he had a degree of prominence, and it was well-known that he was married and already had a family. Eve was so completely smitten with him that she was willing to do anything just to be with him. He sent a servant to accompany her to another country and located a place for her to live. She was well provided for, financially, and had the protection of a lifelong faithful servant. Eve thought the city might be Rome.

Eve had plenty of time on her hands to enjoy the culture, create a home environment, and occupy herself pleasantly while awaiting the arrival of her lover. But the man never arrived to be with her. Eve never doubted his love or that he was trying to return to her. But she had no word from him in all the remaining years of her life. She felt in her heart that he was detained somewhere and was unable even to get a message to her. She passed the time until her death by just getting through each day, one after another. When I asked Eve to identify the man, her servant, and her family, she quickly said, "Oh, the man is Brett! And I think the faithful servant is Ed. He became a friend to me, because we only had each other, and he stayed by me and took care of me." After talking a bit more about her present-day relationship with Brett, and the fact that she worked for him when she was in college, she was still unsure as to why he hadn't returned to her in the days of Greece and Italy. She knew that she was completely faithful to him and eagerly anticipated his return until she died.

In the meantime Geoffrey, a friend of Brett's, also did a regression session with me. He identified himself and Brett as officers in the army of Alexander the Great. Alexander was insatiable in his desire to conquer, loot, and gather treasures. Geoffrey realized that a group of soldiers tried to convince Alexander to cease his campaigns. Everyone was tired, and they hadn't been home to see their families in many years. And it was becoming increasingly difficult to transport all of the treasures Alexander had appropriated for himself. Alexander ordered the group of dissenting soldiers executed. Both Geoffrey and Brett died along with the rest of that group. If that were the case, it would explain why Brett was never able to return to Eve and why he couldn't even get a message to her.

When Eve finished her session, she was amazed at the information that had come from her subconscious. She felt lighter and knew that she had explained a lot about her life through her new awareness. In particular, her relationships with Ed and Brett were completely clear. Regarding her relationship to Ed, she said, "No wonder. It feels like we've always been married, lifetime after lifetime. Even in that life in Rome, he was there to take care of me. It also explains why Ed lets me do whatever I feel is right for me at the moment!" Her relationship with Brett was a bit more complicated, as she has a deep attraction and love for Brett, in spite of her contentment and happy marriage. This situation was beginning to cause some confusion and pain in her life, because Brett hoped she would leave Ed and marry him. Eve had no reason to leave Ed and, in fact, was devoted to her husband, but Brett offered her an exciting life and the kind of passion that convinced her to leave home and family in the Grecian lifetime. In addition to his love, loyalty, and their shared experiences, Ed was the safer choice. He offered her a steady life, whereas some uncertainty would be connected to a life with Brett. Eve understood why she made a clear choice to be with her husband.

Eve and I might never had gone further with the investigation into her past lives if it hadn't been for two factors. Eve's terrible Hitler-Satan dreams got worse. Shortly after our meeting, it was decided that Eve was to accompany me on a five-day conference in another city. I suggested that we do another session while we were at that conference; but a friend who had her best interests at heart had advised her against it, fearing that it might make things worse instead of better. I suggested that we take some time and at least analyze her dream. She agreed.

One evening, after a full day in the conference, we set the stage for the dream analysis. In the process of a dream analysis, I use two chairs so that the person can fully appreciate his inner conflicts as manifested in the dream. As the person moves between the two chairs, he learns how to dialogue with himself. Soon the meaning of the dream becomes clear.

It can often be difficult to keep a person going in such an exercise, especially if he or she considers himself or herself to be psychologically savvy. In the beginning of the exercise, the dialogue is less than scintillating and doesn't seem to go anywhere. It is like getting a piano student to practice scales for half an hour until his fingers are warmed up for the big recital. The seemingly unimportant details that come forth before the real issue breaks loose can seem boring and even ridiculous. But keeping the left brain busy with this exercise allows the right brain to come up with the real information. I use this technique of dialoging with one's subconscious in both dream analysis and regression sessions.

Both Eve and Brett had experienced great frustration in their individual regression sessions with me as I was urging them in the phase of practicing their scales. Just as each one of them was about to get up and tell me they were fed up and finished with this ridiculous procedure, their memory broke through in vivid color and detail. For Brett, this had been especially astounding, as suddenly his sense of smell from a past life was equally as strong as his unexpected visual sense. Eve was just getting to that moment of annoyance in her dream analysis when, with her eyes wide open and staring straight at me, something became very vivid indeed.

I shall never forget the look on her face. Her eyes became wide, frightened, and tearful. She said, "I think I was in Nazi Germany. I see myself with this very handsome man, and I think he betrayed me." As Eve was no longer moving between chairs, I began to ask her the kinds of questions I ask in a regression session, for I had already suspected that the dream analysis would probably lead to a full regression to a past life. In a regression session I ask the person to close his or her eyes, so the present environment will not be distracting. But in a dream analysis the eyes are wide open. Eve was obviously not seeing anything in the room we were in, nor in the present time, even though she was looking right at me. At this point I didn't have to prompt her or ask her any questions, either. I was like a person with dark glasses at a movie theater, with Eve giving me a frame-by-frame description of the movie on the screen.

Eve described herself as a young girl, perhaps fourteen or fifteen years old with the budding quality of great, exceptional beauty in its virginal state. She said, "I look somewhat like I look now, with dark hair, but I'm really a knockout. I have a sophistication that is far beyond my years, and I think I'm older than I really am. I think I really do know it all, and my instincts for flirtation and sexual attraction are all there, even though I haven't had a chance to practice them."

Eve described a garden where people were gathered as if it were a party. But it seemed to have a more serious overtone than just a social situation. She was standing by herself near a hedge, rather bored with the whole thing. As she looked around, she saw a devastatingly handsome man at the bar, getting himself a drink. Within seconds she was walking to the bar to get herself a soft drink as well. They made eye contact, and she had a chance to practice the flirtation that was instinctive. Eve thought that they probably didn't speak to each other just then, but the die was cast. He knew what she was doing, and as they wandered throughout the party, the eye contact continued until they found themselves at the bar again. This time, with very few words, they made arrangements to meet at another time, away from the party. They couldn't speak many words to each other, for if Eve's parents or friends had glanced at them, they would have known in a second what was going on. There seemed to be something else that occupied her parents' attention, and Eve knew it probably had to do with the beginning of the war.

I resisted asking Eve for more details because the look in her eyes told me that something truly frightening was ready to emerge. She needed no help from me. She said, "I become the mistress of this man. I know he is a high-ranking Nazi officer. I see myself at a really elegant party where the men are all very important officers in uniform and the women are really dressed up. I'm wearing a red satin dress." I volunteered, "And ankle strap shoes." She said, "Exactly." I could see what she was wearing and what she looked like as if it were a photograph. Many times, in a regression session, if a person sees an event very clearly, it is like running a film on a screen. I can also see that film.

"I am quite drunk, and I may even take some drugs, occasionally. It feels like it is difficult to keep up the pretense of the situation and this facade. I'm really just a young girl pretending to be a grown-up, and this man is an SS officer, high up in the Nazi hierarchy. He's older and very sophisticated. These other women are the girlfriends of the other officers, not the wives. There are lots of these parties, and I just drink more and more champagne to get through them.

"Oh, my God—I'm Jewish! I feel like I'm betraying my whole family by what I'm doing. But then I rationalize that I'm keeping them safe by being with him. He loves me so much, he'd never let anything happen to them. A part of me is saying, 'I'm not going down with the sinking ship.' But I mainly tell myself I'm helping my family. I think I have a brother and a sister. I'm much closer to my brother. That sister is almost like an inconvenience to me. She might as well be a little brother I don't pay any attention to. My whole family would consider that what I'm doing is so wrong and a real betrayal to them. I feel so guilty."

Eve went on, as if it had happened yesterday. "One day I go home to see my family, and when I get to the apartment, they're not there! Everything is gone, the apartment is empty, cleaned out. I'm devastated, shaken to the core. I race back to him to confront him, and he becomes very angry. He beats me up and says, 'You little Jewish bitch. Who do you think you are? Do you really think you mean anything more to me than a pet dog on a chain?'

"At that moment, my life is over. I don't think I die, but I might as well have died. I'm not there. I've betrayed my family, fooled myself into thinking I could save everyone, and he didn't even love me. I think he gives me twenty-four hours to leave Germany. I don't think I go to a concentration camp. I think I get out somehow. I think my brother comes with me." I ask Eve where they went. She thought a long time and said, "I really don't know. I don't know much of anything after that. We may go to the Orient, but I'm not sure. Everything that happens afterward is completely blank. I just know that somehow my brother is with me. I may be on drugs. I don't know what happens to my father and mother or that sister. She's always been a thorn in my side, but now I feel so guilty about everything. What a fool I've been. I certainly understand why I chose not to be a model or an actress in this life. I consciously chose to develop my mind and become involved in politics!"

Eve and I spent a lot of time on the healing of that experience. Among other healing techniques, I suggested that she figuratively and mentally give comfort to that girl by putting her arms around her. That young girl was really scared, in over her head, and so ashamed. She needed to forgive herself for making a wrong choice in her young life. Eve knew that she'd have to forgive herself, as if she were a mother who never blames her child but only wants to protect. She said, "At least I know that I didn't do anything really evil. I was so afraid from my dreams that I had done something much worse."

To digress for a moment, when Brett knew that I was attending this particular conference, he suggested that Eve come with me. He felt that the conference would give her some new information, and it might be important for a special job he had in mind for her. She happened to tell him she hoped I would analyze her dream/nightmare while we were there. He thought it would be a good idea. Then Brett called me to volunteer something I couldn't have known. As Eve was describing her life in Nazi Germany, I was even more flabbergasted because of what Brett had divulged. Brett was recently divorced but he had been married twice previously, not just once as I had thought.

When Brett was a young man in his twenties, he had met a stunningly gorgeous girl at the Copacabana, a popular nightclub in New York that was one of the places to go in the fifties. After a short engagement, he had a brief marriage to her. Tragically, she was a drug addict. Brett had sent her to a drug rehabilitation center and knew that she would be safe and protected while he was away from New York on a business trip. But while Brett was away, the girl had discovered that she was pregnant, had run away from the center, and had committed suicide. Her life was too far over the edge of horror to think of bearing a child.

Before this gorgeous creature had come to New York, she had been in a concentration camp, and although she was Jewish, she had been the girlfriend of a very high-ranking Nazi officer! Since she was a twin, she had been a victim of Josef Mengele's horrible experiments. The twin sister had been thrown in a fire, and their mother had jumped in after her, leaving Brett's future wife and her brother together in the camp. They survived the war, had been released from the camp, and they were living together in New York when Brett met her. Brett told me a bit more about the situation, but Brett was quite sure that Eve was Bobbi, whom he had married and lost. As Eve was going through her wide-awake regression back to Nazi Germany, I was holding my breath from shock. I remembered her statement before her first regression session with me, "I think I was Brett's first wife!" During the wide-awake session I watched her face, her eyes, the emotion, her tears, and knew this information was all new to her. Brett had not told her his side of the story.

I was sure Eve would hear very little that was being said at the conference the next day. Since Brett was very anxious to know if Eve had confirmed the information about his first wife, I told him what I could without betraying Eve's confidence and trust in me, and I did not tell Eve what Brett had revealed to me. In a situation where two people recall the same scene, I always ask the individuals involved to talk about it between themselves. This way I'm not imposing my thoughts and feelings but asking what they think, and how they see a situation. But I had to swallow hard when I was talking to Brett, because I still felt overwhelmed from the information Eve revealed. I said to Brett, "There are a lot of similarities, but there's enough difference to cast some doubt. You'll have to ask her for the details." Brett and Eve subsequently discussed this session together, but Brett was still reluctant to tell Eve everything he knew about Bobbi, his first wife. He knew that Eve might do more sessions with me, and he didn't want to prejudice her in any way. Brett had also told me that the gorgeous girl he married had just a drop of Jewish blood dating back to the fifth century. The Jewish blood came through Bobbi's mother's side of the family, making Eve and her siblings technically Jewish. The Nazis were meticulous in tracing racial heritage, even back to earlier centuries. I volunteered one more thing. I said, "Eve thinks she and her brother went to the

Orient, not New York." Brett said quietly, "Bobbi and her brother did go the Orient first, and then came to New York."

At a later date, Eve spoke to me on the telephone to tell me what had come into her consciousness after our two sessions together. She began to release information about the time spent in the concentration camp and recalled the horror of the experience. The significant factor that emerged was that Ed, Eve's husband, was her brother in the German lifetime. The closeness that developed was due, not only to the dreadful experiences they shared in the camp, but because Bobbi was a drug addict in that lifetime. Her brother became a drug dealer in order to supply Bobbi. His attitude after the war was so conditioned by what they had suffered, he had no moral judgment about giving Bobbi drugs to help her endure. When Brett first met Bobbi, in his present and Eve's past life, he had no idea about her addiction. When he discovered that she was injecting heroin into the soft tissue between her toes and under her tongue, he was determined to help her kick the habit. She agreed to enter a rehabilitation center outside of New York City, and Roberto, Bobbi's brother, promised to oversee her time there if Brett would go to Turkey to take care of some business for him. Although Brett didn't ask too many questions about the business for Roberto, ostensibly he was to pick up some furniture for their new apartment. Brett decided that Bobbi's future health and well-being would be worth anything he might do in return for her brother's cooperation.

The tragedy for Brett came when he returned to New York from his trip. He arrived at the apartment to find it totally stripped of Bobbi's and his belongings. A note from Bobbi had been left with the concierge of their apartment building. She had left the rehabilitation center only a day after Brett left on the trip, and had decided to end her life. She overdosed on drugs after writing the note to Brett.

In the note, she explained that she had endured such horrors in the camp, she couldn't face life without help from the drugs. More than that, she discovered that she was pregnant. She didn't know whether the baby was Brett's or Roberto's child. When Bobbi and her brother entered the concentration camp, drunken German soldiers forced the siblings to have sex together. The incestuous relationship had lasted throughout their days in camp, as Bobbi would scream uncontrollably at night until Roberto was brought to sleep with her and give her comfort. The incestuous relationship continued until she married Brett, even though both she and Roberto tried to end it.

But now she couldn't be sure whose baby it might be. Bobbi knew that Brett's more sheltered life would ill prepare him for the truth of her experiences during the war. She loved Brett, but she felt that she had to protect him from her devastating experiences in that lifetime. Her loyalty to Roberto, now Ed, was unquestionably deep. Brett was deeply attached to Bobbi, and now Eve. His moral judgment was obviously in the way of his desire to be with her again. Eve's deep sense memory made a life with Brett extremely hazardous. He had abandoned her, unwillingly, in the Grecian lifetime, and she had abandoned him, unwillingly, after the war years.

I stayed in touch with Eve, and am still in contact with her. We obviously made a deep connection with each other throughout the time the past life revelations were coming to mind. Even though the information that came into her consciousness was more horrifying than she could ever have imagined, Eve told me the nightmares had stopped. She said, "Thank you, Counselor." We decided that we would not encourage Ed to do a regression session. Our mutual judgment told us the information might be more than he could assimilate in the present time. If Ed came to me and asked to do a session, that would be different. But it would be against all sense of ethics to suggest that he uncover some memories prematurely.

Eve and Ed have a baby boy now. Eve is very content with her life, and knows that she was really an innocent in the circumstances of the past. Time allows forgiveness to take place. Eve continues to make peace with herself over her sense of betrayal to her family and to Brett, but mostly to herself. She said, "I rarely ever think about this now. I'm free from those terrible nightmares and the pressure to be what everyone expects me to be. I am mostly true to myself, Ed, and our baby. I love Brett with all my heart, and send him loving energy on a silent level. I only wish him happiness in his life. I made a conscious choice, this time, to take a conservative, safe, but correct route in my life. I'm excited about the possibilities for the future. (This story is written in its entirety in *A Soul's Journey*. Many of the details have been edited out in this book.)

Jennifer made an appointment to see me when a short-lived, but very intense, relationship ended. She was in a great deal of pain over a sudden and unexplained separation from someone she loved. She had not seen or heard from the gentleman in question for several years, but she confessed that the experience was so agonizing, she was hesitant to enter into another love relationship at the moment. In the review of her present life, Jennifer brought to light a current relationship with Andre. However, Jennifer had walked away from Andre several times and knew that if she rejected him again, he would not come back. She feared that the unresolved issue with Robert might prevent her from having true happiness with Andre.

Part of her heartbreak was that she had no closure with Robert, for he simply stopped calling her. The cutoff of communications was very abrupt, so Jennifer was never able to tell him how she felt. Robert was certainly holding her at arm's length, if he cared about her feelings at all. The last contact they had was a long-distance phone call just before Christmas, several years before she came to see me. In that conversation, Robert told her that his being able to resolve one financial burden in his life would speed up their being together. He was on his way to the bank at that moment, and asked her to send him lots of good luck. He fully expected that the renegotiation of a tricky real estate situation would be completed that day. Jennifer never discovered the results of his meeting because he never called her again, and ended any calls she made to him very abruptly.

When Robert met Jennifer, he had recently broken up with a girlfriend. He told Jennifer he never wanted to see her or hear her name again. But Jennifer learned that, later on, Robert married Angela after all. It was no solace to learn that he divorced her shortly after their marriage.

Jennifer commented, "If something is so perfect, and one person can't accept happiness, but deliberately chooses unhappiness, how can I trust getting involved again? If I cannot believe words and actions of someone I love, what can I believe? We were so close and so perfect together, the agony of being without him has lasted several years. I just can't believe I was making all that up. I can't believe it was all in my mind."

I suggested that a regression session might heal the wounds and give her some answers. Her description of a former life in Paris, at the time of the French Revolution, was so detailed it surprised me almost as much as it surprised Jennifer.

Before we began her session, Jennifer briefly described meeting Robert. "A mutual friend of ours introduced us over the phone. Our first phone conversation lasted five hours. Robert was financially able to travel whenever and wherever he wanted, so he made arrangements to come to my home to meet me. I was very apprehensive before he arrived, as I sensed this was to be a very special meeting. I wanted everything to be perfect, but I need not have worried. He walked into my apartment and started talking to me as if we had been together all our lives. He was handsome, charming, and everything I could have wanted in a man. From the very beginning, I was attracted to him. He has a wonderful combination of sensitivity, thoughtfulness, and intelligence. He is a man of the world, and yet he is down to earth. He is good-looking, energetic, vital, and sexy. In short, Robert seemed perfect for me.

"We talked for a long time that very first evening. He told me all about himself and the problems he was having in his life. Although he appeared to be financially secure, most of his funds were tied up in a fabulous resort he built. Robert was struggling to stay afloat. I felt tremendous compassion for those real problems, and also for the pain he felt over his divorce. He had been tricked by his ex-wife and her new husband when his wife asked for a divorce. Robert suspected she might be having an affair with a mutual friend, but his wife assured him that nothing was going on between them. Robert even confronted the man he suspected, but was reassured when the friend told Robert they had a mild flirtation, but he loved his own wife and would not dream of breaking up either his own, or another, marriage.

Satisfied that his wife and his friend were telling the truth, Robert agreed to give his wife a large financial settlement.

"As soon as Robert's divorce was final, his former friend got a divorce and married Robert's ex-wife. Robert not only felt duped by them, but since his ex-wife's new husband was extremely wealthy, it was a double-barreled humiliation. On top of all that, the new husband was elected to an important office. Pictures of Robert's ex-wife were constantly appearing on the front pages of the statewide newspapers. Robert was constantly reminded of his naïveté.

"I fell head over heels in love with Robert, with a kind of passion that I had never known before. But a great sadness overtook me as I began to realize the extent of the damage done to him by his wife's betrayal. It was clear that Robert would have difficulty trusting anyone again, and I didn't know how to begin to reassure him. He knew very little about my lifestyle, nor did he ask many questions. I don't think he realized that I led a colorful and eventful life on my own. I was certainly not impressed by his financial status, as I dated many men on that level of success. I just loved to be with him. Eventually I met some of his friends and liked them very much.

"Once Robert took me to an art gallery where I stumbled on a painting that I really admired. The artist was unknown to me, but I was quite taken by the beauty and sensitivity of his work. When I showed the painting to Robert, he questioned my choice by asking, 'Do you really like that?' I stammered a bit and said, 'Well, yes, I think it is very beautiful.' After an apology for 'setting me up,' he told me he owned a painting by the same artist and that it was hanging in his home.

"His testing me about the painting left me puzzled. Was it possible he thought the friend who had introduced us had given me the descriptions of all the paintings he owned? Could he possibly imagine that I had researched the gallery to locate this particular painting so that I could appear to love it to appease him? That incident, among several others, confirmed my fear that his faith in people had been severely damaged, perhaps beyond repair. More importantly, Robert didn't trust his own instincts.

"It was obvious to me that our tastes were the same, but more importantly, our rhythm was the same. We both enjoyed cramming as much as possible into every second of life. To me, our timing was perfect in all respects. We were both always in a hurry, but he was minutes slower than I, which gave me a chance to catch my breath when I was with him. He didn't seem to realize that our being in sync, taste-wise and time-wise, was quite special.

"Although our relationship lasted only a short time, the pain over my lack of contact with him has lasted for many, many years. I wonder if Robert ever knew how much I suffered. Not only my heart, but my body was in great pain, as if part of me had been roughly torn away from another part. My skin actually hurt being away from him. I had never experienced that before nor have I felt anything like it since then."

I directed Jennifer to go to a past life that would help her understand her present-day circumstances. To her surprise, Jennifer saw herself in a life in Paris. She thought it was at the time of the French Revolution. After just a few questions on my part, Jennifer realized she was not only on the side of royalty, but actually lived in the palace at Versailles. She knew she was guillotined along with many other people. A lot of the physical difficulties she had in her present life could be directly related to that time. As a singer in the present time, Jennifer suffers with many sinus and throat problems. The symptoms began when she was a child. She also has a great deal of tension and stiffness around her neck. She was astounded to realize that her vocal problems could be due from the severe wound of being guillotined. She said, "It makes so much sense now. I understand why my singing career has had so many setbacks."

Jennifer flashed on a scene in a lavish room where she was entertaining a lot of people by singing popular, perhaps bawdy, songs. She realized that she hated what she was doing, but continued to smile and appear to enjoy it. She was conscious of living a dual life. She said, "I am being very 'two faced.' I see myself among a group of people who are elegantly gowned and sprawled on chairs and cushions in a gorgeous room. I can envision some of these painted and coiffed people sitting on sofas while others are lounging on silken pillows on the floor. I am standing in the center of that room, on a small raised stage singing 'ditties' to the group. Not all of the people are paying attention as they are talking and gossiping behind open fans, oblivious to what is going on elsewhere in the room. Obviously I am good at entertaining them with my singing. As I finish my song, I am applauded by the men and women closest to me on the floor pillows. Since there is general laughter, I conclude that I must be singing a raucous song that appeals to the sensuality of the men and women. There is nothing wrong with what I'm singing, as long as I sing songs that are in harmony with my thoughts and feelings. However, I sense that as soon as I leave the assemblage, I am very annoyed. I begin to detest these gatherings.

"One of the men in the front of the audience is smoking a long cigarette. Smoking must be a fad new to the court. This man is making broad gestures with his hand so that no one can fail to notice his exceptional good fortune in having tobacco. His self-centered, ingratiating, flirtatious manner is especially irritating, but I see myself responding as if he were my dearest friend and the most scintillating person on earth. This is very funny; I recognized him as an actor who lives in my building. Al often gestures in that same annoyingly theatrical way in the present time."

There were evidently two important men in her life at that time. As we probed a bit farther into her past life, Jennifer saw that she had been widowed when she was very young, but a lover came into her life a bit later on. He was very loyal and faithful to her. She suspected that she knows both men from her life in France in the present time, but she wasn't able to immediately identify them.

Other pictures continued to flash into her mind's eye. As we were talking, she had a glimpse of a small cottage in the French countryside. I asked her to describe it to me, and I suggested that she tell me in present tense, as if she were observing things first-hand.

She said, "I think that cottage is my home. It feels right that I live part of the time at Versailles, but that I have a chance to get away, from time to time, to go to the countryside. I know I can hardly wait to be in a place where it is quiet and peaceful, distanced from the vain people at Versailles.

"I am a different person when I am in my own home. I can relax and just be myself. The house has comfortable furniture and is decorated in soft colors. I love to fill the house with lovely flowers. I see it so clearly. If I were an artist, I could draw a picture of it. I really need the serenity and quiet of the French countryside to soothe my tired nerves, overstrained from the effort of constantly being on guard at court. When I am at Versailles, I am watched by people ready to gossip about me and denigrate me at the slightest provocation. For some reason I seem to be in a position to stir up envy by my slightest action. I don't understand why I am such a target for gossip. Everyone gossips, of course, but it seems I am being watched in particular. It is very difficult to live in that fishbowl.

"I love escaping to my country house. I think I

bring lots of food home with me when I come from the palace . . . hampers full of pastries, game, and exotic dishes . . . so that I can give gifts to my neighbors. These simple folk know I live at Versailles, but they don't care what position I hold. I might be anyone at all, as they take me at face value. They are kind and lovely people. They're very helpful and never pry or ask questions. I genuinely like the people who live close by and who work for me. I admire their simplicity and honesty.

"I believe times are getting more difficult because word is passed along that I have access to extra food. Many people begin coming to my door for something to eat. These people are not interested in fancy fare, they just beg me for anything to fill their bellies. At first it is just a few extra people, maybe relatives of the people who work for me, but soon I can see swarms of people peering at me and trying to come into my kitchen. People start out being very polite and asking for just a little bit of bread. Then some of the men threaten me with physical harm if I don't provide for them. It is clear that these people are starving.

"Even now I can feel how upset I am. I am so sorry for these hungry people, and as more and more strangers begin to gather at my door, I am devastated not to have enough food for everyone. It is just heartbreaking to see so many hungry people, especially if there are children in the crowd. To this day I can't bear to think of anyone being hungry, much less see a picture of a starving child or baby. I give away whatever I have, and I try to explain that I can bring only so much food at one time. I promise to bring more on the next trip, but soon it becomes a real problem. My home is no longer a place of solace and rest.

"Now I am being mobbed by people who demand that I give them something to eat. It is just a nightmare and gets worse as time goes on. I am becoming more and more terrified of the mobs, and eventually I have to barricade the doors. It devastates me to turn my back on them and ignore their pleas. The only thing that saves me is my lover. He either lives with me or meets me when I come home. He is tremendously protective and indispensable in keeping people away. I'm sure they could easily break down my doors. I know I could not keep the doors barred without him, and I suspect I could have been killed.

"There is no longer any joy in coming home or of passing out food for the people I know. I can't feed everyone, and I don't know how to divide things up among so few. So eventually, when I am in the country, I am forced to shut myself away from everyone but my lover. I can't even go outside to walk in my garden. It is a very tense time.

"I think I choose odd hours to travel, and I can see myself huddling against the wall of the carriage trying to hide. I know I am given advance notice, by someone outside of the court, that things are coming to a head among the people of the towns. Rumors have been brewing about the common people taking action against royalty, but no one actually believes it will come to that. There are some of us who are very angry at Louis for not being more decisive. He should address the issues at hand and, at the very least, find a way to pass out bread among the people. He is so weak, he does nothing at all. One day I am warned that it will be very dangerous to remain at Versailles and that I must leave immediately.

"Now I see another very vivid scene. I see myself leaving a building at Versailles, and I can see a particular doorway where I am running out as fast as I can go. I'm in a huge hurry. I can feel my heart pounding so hard you can see the throbbing in my throat. A carriage is waiting, and I am racing as fast as I can down the right side of an outside staircase. There are about four or five steps leading from a small stoop to a flat area, like a driveway, curving down each side of the doorway. Although there are only a few steps, I can feel the heavy train of my dress bumping down those stairs. I am almost panicked because that dress is slowing me down and there is a great urgency to get away as fast as possible. I feel like my heart will jump out of my body.

"My carriage is waiting for me, ready to pull off at a moment's notice, but it is as if I might be stopped before I can even reach the door. The driver is on his seat with the reins in his hands, not down below to help me in. I know I have been told of an impending attack on Versailles. This is my only chance to get away. I don't have time to warn anyone else, and I'm not even sure I think of that. I know I feel very ashamed, later on, when I realize what happens to my friends. I don't know how I have advance information, and I don't know why I am being warned, in particular. There are no other waiting carriages that I can see. It seems to be late morning, and I believe everyone is asleep.

"The ride home is absolutely terrorizing. I stay huddled in the corner of the carriage, as best I can, in hopes that no one will see me or recognize me. My lovely coach stands out like a sore thumb on the rough, rutted roads, and I am being jolted all over the inside of the carriage as my driver ignores the bumps for the sake of speed. There are very rough men on horseback all along the route home. I hold my breath each time we pass a group of people, but I don't think I am stopped. Then, very suddenly, we are not allowed to pass, and I am being pulled from the carriage. As I am being dragged out, very violently, my lover rides up just in time to save me from more harm. Someone knows him and calls him 'the Captain.' The Captain evidently convinces them that I should be spared, that I am not the enemy.

"My lover seems to belong to a different social class than I do; as though he is of good parentage but is not of noble blood. He is probably an officer in the army. I know I never take him to the court. I deliberately keep him away. I'm sure I conceal my relationship with him from the people I associate with at Versailles, as he absolutely wouldn't fit in. I seem to straddle a social line myself. I don't think I am born noble, but of a good solid, upper-class French family.

But I seem to be very wealthy, and I have close friends in high places.

"Oh, I think my marriage is the key to my being at Versailles. My young, handsome husband is a nobleman and takes me to live at Versailles after our wedding. I don't believe he lives very long. I think he is seized by a sudden illness that takes him away from me, for I see myself just devastated by a terrible loss. I can feel that deep sorrow even now. I believe I turn to the church for solace, for I am absolutely inconsolable and alone in that world."

Jennifer paused for a few moments. "There is a woman at court who takes pity on me. She is also terribly lonely and is deeply misunderstood, and we become very best friends. Oh, my God, her name is Marie Antoinette! We develop a deep, lasting friendship." Jennifer was silent as the significance of what she saw began to sink in. "We spend much of our time trying to get away from the intrigues, gossip, and malice that is so prevalent. She is very fond of her husband, but is left alone quite a lot. He bumbles his way through life, but the brunt of things fall on Marie's young shoulders. She is accused of the worst of everything. She is terribly hurt by it all. I believe the reason I am targeted for special gossip is because of my friendship with her.

"I know people are jealous of the small circle of friends we have, and we don't seem to take many pains to conceal our sense of exclusivity. I feel like I walk a terribly fine, dangerous line. Even though we share so much, I feel different in some way. Although

I seem to have plenty of money, and I'm in the inner circle at court, I am also comfortable with the country people. I must have some connection with the townspeople of Paris, as I'm sure someone from the side of the Revolution warns me about the impending danger. That is not quite clear to me, however.

"I do realize that I have a strong spiritual side to my nature and I abhor my own conduct with the phony people at court. I am certainly going against my own nature. I try to appease dangerous or difficult people at court with flattering comments and smiles. I even resort to some level of conspiratorial communication. I should say I gossip, but I am very careful. I am totally loyal to Marie and never allow anyone to say anything detrimental about her.

"I feel as though I am wearing a huge wig, a heavy ornate dress with a train, and carefully applied makeup. I think I have a pleasant, perhaps even beautiful, face. Marie and I spend hours getting dressed and getting made up. I can see ornately dressed men and women sitting in the chairs along a hallway of mirrors. Obviously there is a pecking order, of sorts. I develop a patronizingly friendly way of saying a few words here and there, and I believe I am quite good at disseminating charm and throwing out witticisms, but it is a matter of survival. Now I see a roomful of dancing couples. It is a heady life, and I catch some of the feelings of excitement, even now, that comes just by entering the rooms and absorbing the ambience. I have to admit to myself that I may go through a phase, early on, of some promiscuity and naughtiness. In the beginning, I enjoy the raucous living, but later on all the frivolity becomes tiresome.

"Another vivid scene pops into my mind. I see myself starting down a corridor, smiling and flirting with people sitting on chairs along the way, and suddenly I see Louis, the king, coming toward me. It is too late to turn down another hallway, so I have to curtsy to him and engage in a conversation that is always incredibly boring. I seem to shudder when I see him coming my way because I think he is so weak and inept. I wish that he would defend his wife a bit more. No one in the court dares blame him for anything, so they blame her. She is loyal and good, but young and naive. Our greatest offense toward other people at Versailles is in wanting to go off by ourselves with a few other people who are part of Marie's inner circle of friends. We create amusing diversions to prevent boredom from setting in. Some of those amusements were envied and misunderstood, but we ignore the gossip about our activities.

"Eventually, I can see that I turn away from some of the frivolity. I seem to be occupying my time in a way that isn't appealing to her. I may be going home more often, or going into Paris without her. I cause some small estrangement with Marie by doing so. However, we grow even closer later on after her children are born. Eventually, the bond of friendship becomes very, very strong because of the impending danger. Our friendship commences when we recognize our mutual loneliness and feelings of isolation, as neither of us feel that we belong there. Now, with each bit of bad news, our sense of isolation is intensified. All of the pandering by the courtiers to the king prevents her from spending much time with Louis. Otherwise, she might be able to persuade him to face up to the truth and take action to prevent ultimate disaster. She is particularly lonely because of Louis' weak personality, but she loves him anyway.

"Marie talks Louis into building a haven for her. It is a little hamlet where we can hide. We often take Marie's little daughter with us to play with the lambs and stroll through the lanes. It seems that I became almost like her child's guardian. At the very least, I am as close to the little girl as to her mother.

"It is just a horrible way to live. It might appear glamorous to others, but I am in an especially precarious position because of my friendship with Marie. There are many attempts to sabotage our friendship and discredit me. Fortunately, she always relies on me when the chips are down. No matter what is said in public, we have our own code and always speak very candidly with each other.

"I am aware of some associations with the common folk of Paris, and I know that, in itself, is very unusual. The women of the court usually keep to themselves and do not mingle with the people of Paris. Yet I see myself going into Paris alone, quite often, in disguise. I think I dress simply, leaving my wigs and best gowns behind, and use a plain black coach for travel. I wonder what I might be doing in the city. I certainly **am** leading a double life. Some of the people I know in Paris would be very uncomfortable and completely overwhelmed by the grandeur of the court.

"I don't know for sure, but I believe St. Germain holds classes in Paris for the development of higher consciousness. I believe I attend those classes. St. Germain seems to be a close friend of mine. He is enormously wealthy and influential, but lives a fairly simple life in Paris. I think he was at Versailles for a period of time, and I probably develop a friendship with him there. The group of people that meet at his house are varied. I get to know a girl who is really a high-class prostitute. I think she is of the bordellos in Paris, but entertains gentlemen from the court. She is very metaphysically oriented, in spite of her occupation, and I like her very much. It makes sense that she might be the person who warns me to leave Versailles. I can now see her as part of our group studying with St. Germain. She lives in the heart of Paris and never sets foot in the court. She has the ear of several gentlemen of the court who are her patrons, and she is in touch with everything going on in Paris as well. Everyone keeps her well-informed.

"I can sense how my behavior changes, as news of the situation begins to filter through the impenetrable wall of pomposity throughout the court. Although it is no longer safe to travel to Paris, my acquaintance from St. Germain's classes manages to keep me abreast of the situation. The courtiers are in complete denial of the level of unrest in Paris and become even more disdainful of the people's cries.

Finally I know our reckless abandon will be the cause of our undoing. There have been plenty of warning signs, but the tide of indulgence prevented anyone from hearing bad news. No one paid any attention.

"Frivolity continues to sweep everyone along, lending a sense of false protection from the anger of the people. I can feel a poignant level of friendship that deepens between a select few of the women. We stop being rivals for the queen's affections. Even though we are all so frightened, we take time to give as much comfort to each other, and try to muster up. My friend Helena is among that close-knit group. Her friendship in the present life is much the same as it was in France. I can see my friend Sonya there, too. Oh, Sonya is one of the friends I met through Robert in this lifetime.

"I know, with great certainty that I spend a lot of time in the white and gold chapel on my knees, fervently praying to God. I pray that we would be granted safety, and I pray for courage. I suspect that I heal some of my less-noble acts of that life through my intense and sincere prayer. The church becomes both my solace and a place where I can struggle with my terror. I go into that holy atmosphere and let out all my fear through frantic prayer and torrents of tears. There is little comfort from the abbé, but what I learned under the tutelage of St. Germain becomes some sort of wellspring of strength. I can see myself struggling between times of panic and terror to moments of finding inner strength. I keep trying to reach a higher source of courage.

"With advance warning from the girl in Paris, and the help of my lover, I get away before the bloodbath of the Revolution begins. After I escape from Versailles, I believe I leave France altogether and am totally safe. I evidently say good-bye to my lover, and I think he is devastated at my leaving him, yet he knows I must get out of France if I'm to be safe. But I also know I am eventually guillotined, so that doesn't make any sense. I don't know how that occurs."

That was about as much information as Jennifer was able to reveal to herself at one sitting, but she was stunned to know that so much detail could emerge into her conscious mind. I felt she had enough for one day, and I suggested that she call me if, or when, she wanted to go further into the details of that lifetime.

After making another appointment a few weeks later, Jennifer told me that a great deal of information had come into her consciousness, especially when she wasn't thinking about our regression session. The most important revelation that came to her was about Robert, for she placed him in the French lifetime.

Jennifer began by saying, "It didn't take long for me to discover that Robert was my husband in that life. He was of royal blood, and I believe we fell in love after a chance meeting in Paris. I'm born into a fine family with a lovely home in the city. I see my-self in a little shop that I own. I'm selling things like bonnets and ribbons just to occupy myself. I'm slated for a 'good' marriage, but when Robert proposes to me, it is beyond my wildest dreams. I am suddenly catapulted into a society that is extremely heady and exciting. My wedding takes place at court. I am the envy of all the young women of noble blood who might have married him. They probably resent the fact that he picks me, a commoner, instead of some-one on his own social level. Interestingly enough, Robert enjoys being in touch with the townspeople. Perhaps he also needs to get away from the stuffiness of the court.

"Being catapulted onto that level of society must be very difficult for me, for I don't think I am pre-pared to live in an atmosphere of intrigue, gossip, scandal, and betrayal. Robert doesn't take anyone at court very seriously, but I am on my toes all the time. I'm very conscious of not being royal. It must be hu-morous, and sometimes irritating to him, to see that I am trying so hard to fit into the social scene, but he tries to be very supportive. He is my love and my protector. After he dies, I am extremely lonely. The loss is just devastating, because I love him with all my heart. I not only miss him, but I think I am very hurt that he leaves me to face life alone. He is my only real link to the court, and now I am stuck in this difficult lifestyle because of him. I think I even be-come angry with him, after his death, just to hide some of my grief. I'm way over my head in trying to deal with the politics of the court. I have to learn the fine art of proper court formality. It is essential not to offend anyone by a chance look or by forgetting to flatter when it is expected."

Jennifer had an amused smile on her face when she said, "This is so unbelievable. One major period of time, in my present life, has reflected so much of what happened then. It is almost like a carbon copy of people and events, but the order was somewhat reversed in the present time.

"I also recognize my current boyfriend, Andre, from the French lifetime. He was the Captain. Our situation is exactly the same in this life as it was before. We don't live together all of the time, in the present, and I'm not sure about marrying him in this lifetime, either. I hesitate to include him in a great deal of my social life in the present, as was true with the Captain in the former life. The Captain never went to court with me. In the present life, I do include Andre in some special situations, but mostly I lead one life with him and a completely separate life without him. He really adores me, and is there for me in all ways in both lifetimes. At one point, I moved to California and left him behind. I did not even suggest that he go with me. But eventually I came home again, and resumed my relationship with him."

I suggested to Jennifer that her relationship with Robert might have been doomed from the beginning because of the patterns of the past. I suggested that in retrospect, and on a soul-consciousness level, he might still harbor some guilt about leaving her so ill prepared for what she eventually had to endure. He would be especially careful about propelling her into a different lifestyle than what she appeared to have. He might even worry about exposing her to danger. I explained to Jennifer that the level of awareness would have remained on a soul-consciousness level, not in his conscious mind. If I had been able to regress Robert as well as Jennifer, the wounds might have been healed and new levels of awareness could replace resistance on Robert's part. Jennifer confessed that she argued with Robert a great deal. She said, "I finally had to admit that I was angry with him a great deal of the time. No doubt that prevented our being together again. Afterward, I was sorry that I didn't express more compassion for his problems. I think I was still angry for his dying in the French lifetime. Clearly that anger was a cover-up for the devastating sadness and loss I felt.

"After his silence, I had recriminations about some of the things I said. I was trying to bolster him, instead of really consoling him. I need to apologize to him for being angry before. I certainly need to reassure him that he is not responsible for what happened to me, later on. It was my choice to remain at court. I could have gone back to Paris and away from the court altogether.

"I think Robert assumed I would be impressed by his lifestyle. He didn't know about the kind of experiences I had before I met him. For many years I spent a great deal of my time with a friend of mine who married an extremely prominent man in New York society. He was a restaurateur extraordinaire. He was also French. In New York City, like few other places, a successful restaurateur is like a king. This man was the king of the kings in a circle that included many grand balls and gourmet dinners. He and my friend had a very beautiful estate outside of New York City, where his closest friends gathered every weekend. There were the 'regulars' and there were guests. The closest friends of this popular couple were the ones who could pitch in and help prepare the feasts that took place all weekend long. The meals were simple, but elegant, and each course was accompanied by the finest rare wines. The decor of the home was luxurious with priceless antiques everywhere. However, it was very comfortable. Guests wore blue jeans and casual clothes until Sunday night, when everyone dressed for dinner. Then the quite beautiful daily tableware was replaced by rare china and brilliant candelabra.

"Discussions were always interesting and stimulating. As I would gaze around the beautiful table where internationally known people were in attendance, I often wondered how I happened to be there, for I was a regular. My presence was due to the insistence of my friend, Helena, for I had never insinuated myself into such a scene. Naturally, my social life in New York took on a rare glow, as I was also included in dinners at the finest restaurants in the city. I was always at the country estate on weekends, and it was like being in a miniature Versailles. It was certainly more elegant and refined than the ostentatious glitter of the court. I began going to the estate for the first time when I suffered a very difficult loss in the present time. My friend Helena took pity on me in this life as she did before."

Helena's husband was building a huge resort, which he eventually lost. The circumstances were very unusual, and there was a suspicion of sabotage. Jennifer volunteered, "Perhaps he was Louis, who lost a kingdom, not just a resort. I never told Robert about that phase of my life, and he had no way of knowing that I was quite used to the most glittering and luxurious surroundings. I suspected there was no way I could tell him about anything that happened to me in the past, as he would immediately think I was being grandiose. It might have seemed to be a put-down.

"In my present life, a friend of Robert's, named Suzanne, made a special effort to make me feel welcome. When we met, she was working on a needlepoint canvas. I was prompted to tell her that I also loved to needlepoint. Her response stunned me. She said, 'Oh, we probably perfected our needlepoint while we were waiting in jail to be guillotined at the time of the French Revolution.' Then she quickly added, 'Oh, I didn't mean that.' But I knew she did, and I also knew she was probably quite correct about her assumption.

"At a later date, when I was attending the metaphysical conference in the town where she lived, I happened to introduce her to Pauline. Suzanne, who was so warm and friendly to me, froze upon meeting her. She was suddenly cold and distant, and I was shocked. I knew that they had both lived during that time in France, and I thought they would like each other. Finally, the air was so frosty Pauline said, 'I don't think Suzanne likes me very much.' Suzanne's reply was, 'You were the one who caused my death on the guillotine in France. Oh, I didn't mean that.' But she did. Pauline had fingered her at the time of the Revolution.

"When I first visited Versailles in this life, and walked down a long corridor, I could sense what it was like to live in the palace. Although I had never been to Paris in this life, nor had I read very much about the French Revolution, I knew what had happened, of course, even though I didn't know exact details. I had read about Versailles and knew that it was built by Louis XIV. I was aware that it was an extravagant plan that almost bankrupt the economy during his reign, but I was not acquainted with the size of the land, nor the layout or the variety of buildings. I was not even sure about how the palace looked from the outside. I wanted to go to Paris to see for myself, but I was also reluctant to confront my fantasies.

"An opportunity arose one summer for a visit to Paris. A group of people had invited me on a special trip to do a seminar about my work in the theater. At the last minute I declined the offer and greatly offended the people who had arranged my visit. I was sorry to let them down, but for some reason, I was very frightened of visiting Paris. I had already bought an airline ticket, and eventually I felt compelled to use it before it expired. Another opportunity for a trip arose when a young friend invited me to her wedding in Paris. Katherine had come from Paris for a visit with friends in New York, and to announce her engagement to a successful, young French photographer. Since she invited me to visit her in Paris, I decided to use my ticket and go to Katherine's wedding. Katherine had been living with her photographer fiancé for some time, so there would be no immediate honeymoon trip for them. She told me she would have plenty of time to spend with me in Paris.

"My flight was to leave on Sunday afternoon. On Saturday, the day before the flight, I was so ill with a high fever and a very sore throat that I remained in bed all day long. It was difficult to even contemplate packing much less taking a trip the next day. However, my ticket would expire if I didn't go ahead with my plans. I decided that I could always sleep on the plane and stay in bed in my Paris hotel room, if it were necessary. At least I would be there for my friend's wedding.

"My terror of actually going to Paris for the first time increased. However, Katherine was anxiously awaiting my arrival. Throughout the day in bed, I admonished myself for causing such an illness through my imagination. I didn't have an ordinary sore throat, I had a sore soft palate. The pain went across my throat instead of up and down. Since I already had the idea that I was guillotined in that life, I felt utterly foolish to have pain where my head might have been taken off. There is really no way of describing the panic and fear that took hold of me as I lay helpless in bed that day. With sheer effort of will, I got up on Sunday and put some things in a suitcase. I steeled myself for the trip. In the past, if I ever traveled with a slight cold, the plane ride itself was torture.

"To my amazement, this trip across the ocean was very pleasant. As soon as dawn broke over the European continent, I felt a new sense of excitement. The sore throat and fever disappeared. When I stepped off the plane at O'rly Airport, the first of many interesting adventures began. There were lots of parties given by friends to celebrate the marriage. In the daytime Katherine and I explored Paris. We walked in the Tuileries, where I felt totally at home. It was as if I had walked there many times in the past. I knew my way around Paris without looking at a map, and never felt lost. When Katherine and I walked through the Louvre, we fantasized about a certain staircase. We sensed that we had lived there before it was a gallery. Katherine insisted she was only a little girl, but I knew I was a young woman. I could feel my train bumping down those stairs again. The drive around the Conciergerie was frightening. I learned at a later time that was the building where prisoners were kept until they could be guillotined. The conditions at the time of the Revolution were far from sanitary, the food was disgusting, and I could imagine being inside that building with rodents running all over my feet and body. I have been terrified of those creatures from childhood to this very day. It doesn't matter if they are small and cute or if they are the larger variety. I become frozen with fear if I see one, dead or alive. I had already traced my fear to that time and place.

"Finally, we planned a visit to Versailles. I almost didn't get there at all, as the days and nights were full of planned activity. Katherine and her new husband, Jacques, along with Jacques' parents, were going to drive me to the palace. We finally set off the day before I was to fly home to New York. I was full of anticipation and foreboding. I wanted to prove to myself whether all the senses and visions had been mere fantasy or whether I really did have a life in the French court. I decided the proof of the pudding would be to find 'my doorway' ... the one from which I had escaped.

"I was quite let down as I saw Versailles for the first time. It was huge, imposing, and the wrong color. There could be no doorway here, such as I had imagined. As we toured through the palace, it felt comfortable and familiar, but I was feeling disappointment, yet some relief, in not finding the special place that had great meaning to me. The corridors of Versailles were just as I had envisioned them before.

"The white and gold chapel was very familiar. I could sense, for the first time, how terrified we must have been as the rumors from the towns and countryside grew. As I reexperienced all this in a flash, standing in the chapel at Versailles, I could understand my reaction to the Catholic church in the present time. When I would accompany my husband to Mass, I would feel such anguish and pain, I could hardly stay through the ceremony. I had never understood why I had such anguished reactions to Catholic rituals, but I understood now.

"During my visit to Paris, I had shared my fantasies and inner experiences about living during the time of the Revolution with both Katherine and her new husband. Neither were very surprised, and they accepted what I told them without any skepticism. The newlyweds had a small house in the country near the town of Versailles. Jacques told me about another house, nearby, that was quite old and had an original thatched roof. He said, 'I think that was your house.' If there had been more time, they might have taken me to see that house. I had hoped I could see it, if only to know for myself if it really was my house from that lifetime. I would have been totally honest with myself if it had not been my former home. I've tried to push away excess imagination with every other bit of investigation about this lifetime, and I have nothing to prove to anyone else . . . only to myself.

"As we continued our tour around the palace grounds new feelings of intense emotion began to take over random thoughts in my mind. We wound our way toward Trianon, a smaller palace Louis built for Marie Antoinette. It was pink, round, and not at all like the building where 'my door' had been. Katherine said, 'I know what you're remembering,' and hurried me through Trianon down a pathway toward Le Petit Trianon. I had seen pictures of this charming palace taken from the garden side of the building, but I had never seen a picture of this exposure.

"A fence and hedge were hiding the facade of the palace from view. As I approached what I now know was Marie Antoinette's special little palace, and the location of her theater, I stopped in my tracks, and with pounding heart I said, 'If I see my doorway beyond this fence, I might really faint. I'm suddenly feeling very weak.' There were several roads converging in front of that building that looked like any other roads. I indicated to Katherine and Jacques that the road going straight ahead looked exactly like the road where the carriage took me on my escape from Versailles. I asked Jacques to show me the specific road that led to their country house. He pointed down the road I had indicated and said, 'Straight down that road.' I found my legs again and continued to walk toward the spot where we were to meet Jacques' parents with the car. As I passed the end of the fence, I found my door . . . the one leading into Le Petit Trianon. It was exactly as I had seen it in my mind's eye, even to the steps and circular driveway where my carriage had waited. I found the confirmation I needed to believe all I had seen and sensed was real.

"Katherine grabbed me by the hand and continued to lead me down the path beyond the building I had seen so vividly in my mind's eye. Jacques was calling to her to come back. He was sure we would be gone too long and keep his parents waiting. She pulled me onward anyway. As we ran, we looked over our shoulder to see if the car had arrived. We both felt we had done this a thousand times before. It seemed we would run toward Marie Antoinette's hamlet, looking over our shoulder to see if anyone spotted us, or was following us.

"The day at Versailles ended, but my inner adventure did not. A mystery still remained. I knew without doubt that I had escaped from Versailles in my carriage. I now had seen for myself, in real life, the very doorway and road of my inner vision. I also knew I had been taken to Conciergerie to await my execution, and I could see the horror of walking through a crowd of jeering people to climb onto a platform housing the guillotine. I knew I had been killed. But how did I happen to be caught once I had escaped from the palace?

"Quite some time after my one and only trip to Paris, I found a book about Marie Antoinette. I learned that she did, indeed, have a little theater with scheduled performances that were held at Le Petit Trianon for only a very select few people at the court. Marie Antoinette had a best friend, the Princess de Lamballe, who had escaped from Versailles just before the palace was stormed and had gone to another country for safety. However, the princess's loyalty to Marie was so strong, she returned of her own volition to be at Marie's side during the last days of their lives. The king and queen were housed in a building overlooking the Tuileries, a large park in the middle of Paris. That building was later used as an art gallery and was called the Louvre. That is where Princess de Lamballe joined the king and queen until the time of her death. As an added torture for Marie Antoinette, the princess was guillotined before her. The severed head was placed on a spike and paraded in front of the apartments where Marie and Louis remained, now alone with each other at last. Many more facts, that had been part of my inner journey, were confirmed by information in the book.

"My friend, Katherine, had one more experience that filled in more of the picture of our life together at that time. I had suggested that Katherine do a regression session to see what details might emerge. Katherine had been reluctant, so I didn't push the issue. However, the three of us . . . Katherine, Jacques, and I . . . had gone on a skiing trip to Colorado, as Jacques was an avid skier.

"Prior to that trip Katherine had a serious accident, breaking her neck. It was due to Jacques' quick thinking that she was saved from a severed spinal column. She wore a neck brace for a year after that time, and she was unable to ski on this trip. One evening at dusk, Katherine and I were alone in the kitchen of the cottage where we were staying. Katherine was in a pensive mood and was standing by a window looking at the snow. I asked her quite innocently, 'What are you looking at?' Katherine replied, 'A courtyard,' and continued unraveling a scene from her mind about her last days in France at the time of the Revolution.

"Katherine just started talking, and I just listened to what she said. She described her role as Marie Antoinette's daughter. She talked about her brother and about their being executed. She expressed her terror at being taken away from her mother and being led toward the guillotine. She said, 'I have been trained as a princess not to show my emotions in front of strangers, so I'm very dignified on the surface. Inside, I'm trembling but staying strong at the same time. As they lead me up the stairs to the platform, I allow myself to look at the crowd below. Then I catch sight of you. You are crying so hard that I can't stay aloof any longer. You are very special to me. Your reaction to my death unnerved me completely. It was then more traumatic than it might have been otherwise. We were so close to each other.'

"One more incident occurred in relation to that lifetime. I was in a midwestern town attending a workshop and went to visit a local metaphysical bookshop. I talked to the owner of the shop at great length, and he even joined me for lunch at a later date during a break from the workshop. As we talked, we identified each other from the lifetime in France at the time of the Revolution. He told me, and I knew, that he was my executioner. I remembered that he had tried to be as kind as possible when I was under the guillotine. He was only doing his job. We parted amicably, but I was left with a very sick feeling in the pit of my stomach for quite a few days afterward.

"After my return to New York, I continued to study voice with fine teachers, but I understood that having a singing career was not the prime reason for my passion for my vocal studies. Deep wounds were imbedded to my esoteric body, especially around the area of my throat, as a result of my beheading. I have thyroid problems in the present life, and what is called a 'military neck.' That is, the neck goes straight up into the head instead of having a gentle curve. My sinus problems and an excess of phlegm that accumulated on my vocal cords began to be alleviated as time went on. Evidently some inner direction led me to continue with the vocal lessons in order to heal those wounds. The vibration of sound and music is one of the greatest healing methods of all.

"Katherine's accidental breaking her neck also focused on a weakened area of her body. For both of us, many phobias and fears were released as a result of our mutual experiences.

"I devoured every book I could find about karma, and how it develops from lifetime to lifetime. As these pictures flashed before me, it seemed perfectly logical that I was unconsciously trying to balance the scales from that time to the present by denying myself the pleasure of having a successful musical career in the present. I was, no doubt, actively punishing myself two centuries later for being two-faced, as well.

"I was later told by a psychic, who knew nothing of my own vision, that I was actually stopped and pulled from the carriage. She said my lover rode up just in time and saved me from harm. She said I called him the Captain. My lover at that time was Andre, my mate in the present time. Our situation was exactly the same in that life. Andre and I were not married in that life nor in the present, but my love for him was then, and is now, very strong and deep. He filled an important void in both lifetimes, it seemed.

"In this lifetime I have an insatiable desire to read every metaphysical book I can find. I am especially fascinated by St. Germain, and I have researched a great deal about his life. He was a man who appeared to be in his young to middle years, yet the rumor was that he was actually very, very old in spite of a very youthful appearance. At first I read about his theories on alchemy and manifestation. Later I read historical accounts about his life at Louis XVI's court. He was appointed minister of war by Louis, but that appointment didn't last very long. No one wanted to hear about how the indulgence at the court was affecting the people of Paris. No one wanted to talk to the common people, or find appeasement. St. Germain left his post, but retained influence as a man of wealth and stature living a luxurious life in Paris. He might have been able to change history to avoid the Revolution, but he couldn't get the attention of the weak king who appointed him. He was able to smooth over a nasty incident involving Marie Antoinette and a diamond necklace, however, and he remained in the good graces of their majesties."

Many years later, Jennifer contacted me to explain the inner growth she experienced as a result of her sessions with me.

"The full experience of my life in France took place over many years. Periodically something would happen to release new remembrances, or I would meet someone who I knew had been with me at that time. My ability to tune into the situation was so real, I never doubted that it had taken place. I just know too many details about that life. I have been able to resolve my painful separation from Robert, and now I only wish him the greatest joy and happiness in all his endeavors. I may never marry Andre, yet I'm so grateful for knowing and loving him in both lifetimes.

"My greatest desire now is to share my knowledge, learned at the feet of St. Germain. I am eagerly awaiting all opportunities to do so."

Needless to say, Jennifer radiated abundant joy and enthusiasm after her inner adventures and memories as the Princess de Lamballe at such an eventful time in history.

CHAPTER 5

Past-life violence; fears and repression in the present.

It is surprising to note that when violence has occurred in a past life, the people involved are drawn back together again in close association in the present, as if they were two prizefighters in a ring. Sometimes the former victim returns with antipathy they can't explain, and yet it is impossible to walk away from the individual they fear. This can often occur in parent-child associations, as an example. The child might be unreasonably worried about antagonizing the parent, but the opposite can also be true. A parent might have a hidden agenda with one or more of his children. Unfortunately, the fear may also be a magnet that attracts two people in a love relationship, which proves to be anything but loving.

It would be logical to assume a subtle kind of recognition would take place, repelling a former victim. The opposite reaction is more evident, however. It has often been observed by therapists and social workers that if there is a suspicion of child abuse by parents, it is fairly easy to determine which parent has been the perpetrator. The child usually goes to **that** person, rather than the innocent parent, as if to say, "Please love me." Rejection, abuse, violence, and abandonment often act like a magnet in relationships, whereas it would seem logical for the opposite to be true. The same pattern of attraction to abuse exists from lifetime to lifetime.

John saw himself in a lifetime where he tried to save a woman and child from being robbed or raped. He saw himself on a London street, on a foggy night, observing some kind of attack by a man. John had a gun, so he shot the man to stop him from committing a crime. His aim was good, so he only wounded the man in the left arm, and the woman and child were safe. In the present life, John was born with a small deformity. His left arm was out of alignment at the shoulder and was slightly shorter than the other. After a childhood operation, the difference was not very noticeable. As time went on, John was able to conceal any vestiges of a deformity in his work as an actor. But John lived with this small disadvantage every day of his life and was, quite naturally, conscious of the way he used his arm. After his regression session, John was astounded to realize that he had set in motion a "wounded" arm as a self-punishment for having hurt another human being. The most startling revelation to John was that he was born to the same man he had wounded. It is not hard to imagine what a very difficult relationship existed between John and his father in the present life. A healing occurred as a result of John's new awareness. He discovered that he was automatically less self-conscious of his body. Then, instead of resenting his father for what had appeared to be rejection in childhood, John silently asked for forgiveness. A new rapport developed between John and his father.

When Patricia came to me for a regression session, she was in great pain over the ending of her marriage to a man she still loved deeply. Even though she had been divorced for many years, she felt continuing sadness over the loss of her dream. Patricia was married to Harry for seven years, but she felt Harry never really loved her enough to make a real commitment. When Patricia reviewed her wedding day, she began to cry. She said, "I was so humiliated. When it was time to cut the wedding cake during the reception, Harry was nowhere to be found. We finally discovered him outside, on the grounds of the country club, playing Frisbee with his friends. I was so embarrassed, but I don't believe anyone else thought anything about it. When I look back over the whole wedding day, poor Harry looked like a little boy being dragged to the doctor. Although we stayed married for seven years, I now realize he left me long before I finally gave up. I never saw the relationship for what it was as long as I was married, but I finally had to face facts. Harry is an alcoholic, and I could do nothing about our situation no matter how hard I tried. Now my dream is gone.

"We have a seven-year-old daughter, and I am as sad for her as I am for myself. In a way, she seems to handle the situation better than I do. I wish I knew why I can't just get on with my life. Although I've been divorced for some time, and I certainly don't want to go back to that situation, I can't seem to meet anyone else. Part of me is reluctant to ever marry again."

When Patricia went back to childhood, she told me about a continuing sexual relationship she had with her cousin, starting from the time she was seven years old until she was fourteen. Patricia was stuck in a no-win situation, for she felt she had no choice but to give in to the demands of her cousin, even though she didn't want it to happen in the first place. Patricia's mother worked during the day, and Patricia was left at her aunt's house every afternoon after school. Her boy cousin was about four years older than she. After school, they would go to his attic room to play until Patricia's mother came to collect her. At first her cousin simply wanted to fondle her. Since she looked up to this boy, she allowed him to do whatever he liked. Patricia admitted that she derived some pleasure from being touched. If nothing else, she was getting some much needed attention from someone. A part of her knew what she was doing wasn't right, but she was unable to say no. She couldn't tell her mother because she was afraid of her mother's anger. In truth, she couldn't even hint that anything was wrong. She knew her mother had to work and there was nowhere else she could stay.

Patricia realized that she started setting up a downward trend of helplessness when she was only eight years old. Unfortunately it was all too easy to recognize the same kind of helplessness in her marriage. I asked Patricia to evaluate the level of guilt she felt over the situation with her cousin. She said, "One hundred percent, of course." I asked Patricia if she felt she had done all she could to keep her marriage together. She said, "For years I thought that I should be better, or more loving, or more patient . . . or something. I thought if I was different, my marriage would work." I suggested that she might still feel that way about other issues in her life, but perhaps on a very subtle level. She replied, "Well, not on such a subtle level at all! I feel that way about almost everything." I was very hopeful that Patricia could trace the feelings of helplessness and inadequacy to their roots.

When Patricia went back to a past life, she saw herself on a boat that seemed to be a pleasure vessel. She said, "This is what I'm getting. I'm seeing a boat that has a lot of people on it, and it seems that everyone is staying on this boat for several days at a time. It appears to be the 1800s. It feels as if we are traveling down the coast between England and France on a pleasure cruise. I see myself as a young boy in my early teens. I'm wearing long pants and a cropped jacket with big buttons, and I have on a little cap. The shirt is white with a round collar. My mother is wearing a gray, or blue, long dress with a tight bodice and long skirts, and she is carrying a parasol and a small reticule. My father is there, too, and we all seem to be well dressed. Evidently, we are fairly affluent. I think my father is a doctor. I have a little sister also. She is dressed in a little dress with a long skirt, and she's wearing a bonnet." I asked Patricia how old she lived to be in this life. She replied, "I think I'm only twelve years old when I die. I think the boat sinks, and we all drown." After taking some time to let the circumstances of that lifetime sink in, I asked Patricia to take a look at the people around her. It might be possible to identify someone in her present lifetime. Patricia replied, "I think my father in that life is my father in the present time. I think my mother from that time is my young daughter now. Could that be right? Isn't that funny? I don't think I know my little sister in the present life." I asked Patricia if she felt any responsibility for her family's tragedy. She answered, "Oh, yes, of course." When I asked her why she should feel that responsibility, she replied, "I seem to be a strong swimmer, but it happened very fast, and I'm not close to where my family are sitting. I blame myself for not getting to them in time to save them. Obviously, I couldn't even save myself. So the helpless feeling started even then." I asked Patricia if she has any breathing problems in this day and time. She replied, "I have asthma. Of course, there is a connection. No wonder."

Although the lifetime Patricia reviewed explained a great deal about her feelings of helplessness in the present, and described her health problems, it didn't seem to explain the relationship she has with her mother in the present time. For Patricia does not feel close to her mother now. In fact, although Patricia is an adult, she still has some vestiges of fear toward her mother. Patricia described an early incident when she first felt helpless and afraid of her mother in the present lifetime. She was only an infant, but her mother dropped her. Fortunately, Patricia landed on a soft rug and was uninjured.

I directed Patricia to go to another lifetime that might explain her present-day relationship with her mother. She answered, "Why am I not getting anything?" I suggested that she continue to direct her thoughts toward a life that would give meaning to her present situation. Finally she said, "It looks like an Indian lifetime. It appears to be in the Southwest. I'll just tell you what's popping into my head. I'm a female, and I'm grown up. I might be about thirty years old, and I'm with a group of people, perhaps numbering about forty in all. I have a baby, a little papoose, under a year old, and I have a very loving marriage. I don't think I live to be very old, perhaps only about another five years. I see the baby as a young child now. We are not a nomadic tribe, but we do look for new territory, periodically.

"I think we are attacked by the white man. It seems to be an army that comes upon us, and it is a big surprise. We're not at all prepared, so we can't really defend ourselves." Patricia had a horrified look on her face and said, "Oh, no. Everyone is killed. It's a real massacre. The white soldiers are very brutal. I'm attacked by someone with a knife. He stabs me in the throat. The horrible part is that my child is killed before my very eyes. They cut off her head with the knife. It is so horrible, I don't even want to live. I die shortly thereafter, almost in the same way." Patricia is stunned with the realization of the brutality of the murders. After a while I asked Patricia to take a look at the face of the soldier who killed her and her baby. Tears began to pour from Patricia's eyes. She said, "Yes, I know the person in this life. I know he is now a female." Then Patricia said, "I feel like I'm making this up, but it seems to be my mother in this life, and I know that Harry is my baby."

After Patricia had a chance to digest this new information, she said softly, "Wow! No wonder I feel so responsible for Harry and can't let him go. No wonder I'm still afraid of my mother." Patricia and I discussed how strange it was to be born to the very person who had killed her in a previous life. I asked her if she had a sense of why that happened. She replied, "I suppose it's to give both of us a chance to get it right in this life. As her child, my mother would have to love me, at least a little bit. She may have to learn to forgive herself for the past, even though she's not consciously aware of any of this. I suppose my job is to tell her that it's all right and that I forgive her! When I look at this objectively, I'm sure she was doing her duty, and I'm sure that the white soldiers were frightened of all Indians. I'm not sure why she had to be so brutal, however."

After a short time Patricia continued. "This really does explain why Harry is like my child again, and why he is an alcoholic. If the pictures of such brutality exist in his subconscious mind, no doubt he tries to drown them out however he can. I think I can let him go now, and wish him well. I will have to

work on forgiving my mother, but I also need to acknowledge my actions in this lifetime when I de-
ceived her. From this perspective, it may be that I
was trying to get even with her by doing something
that would have upset her terribly, even if she'd
never found out about it. What a tangled web.

"Actually my mother must have felt terribly upset, on a totally unconscious level, when she saw
who she had given birth to. She couldn't have been
very happy about it. No wonder she dropped me
when I was a baby." I asked Patricia if she thought
her mother had unconsciously, but deliberately, tried
to injure her in this life. She replied, "No. I don't
think so. But my mother didn't seem to be very
strong. That made me even more fearful as a little
girl. I doubted her ability to care for me. No wonder I
didn't feel safe as a child and felt helpless. I don't
have to feel helpless anymore."

The pattern of attraction to a negative, violent past
life emerged again when Sam and Elise came to see
me. The revelation of their past lives was was quite a
surprise to all of us.

Elise is a beautiful young woman with great warmth
and gracefulness. Sam is a charming, cosmopolitan
man. They live in a major East Coast city. Sam came
to the United States from a European country when
he was in his early twenties. His goal was to establish a lifestyle he could only imagine in his native
land, as he emigrated from an area controlled by a
communist regime. He found a job that needed few

qualifications and began to drive a taxicab in New York City, while he perfected his English.

Sam was born with good taste and a strong business sense. With good energy and strong ambition, he was determined to make it to the top of the ladder of success. By working day and night, it didn't take long before he was able to graduate from the tedium of driving a taxi to owning his own business. He met a woman who worked in an upscale midtown office, wooed her, and persuaded her to be his bride. They soon had two beautiful daughters. Before Sam reached the age of forty, he was able to purchase a town house in a very beautiful part of the city and create an extremely comfortable lifestyle for his family.

If one could photograph Sam's life from the outside, it would appear to be an ideal story of success. Sam is handsome, his wife is attractive and well dressed, and his two daughters typical of intelligent, well-groomed, interesting American girls. However, behind the scenes, Sam was miserable. No matter what luxuries he was able to provide for his family, it never seemed to be enough. Although his daughters adored him, he felt totally unappreciated by his wife. Worse than a lack of acknowledgement for his efforts, his wife taunted him. She constantly reminded him of the background he couldn't escape, and kept him under her thumb of constant criticism. Sam hated himself for his inability to stand up to her. He moved out of their bedroom to sleep in the den, but couldn't bring himself to leave his home and family that he had worked so hard to bring together. He even sent his wife and daughters on lavish vacation trips, but declined to join them. He preferred to remain behind, where he could find momentary peace and quiet.

Sam did what many men might do in the same situation. He found solace in a pair of lovely arms. The woman of his choice was Elise, a sweet, gorgeous, blond European model. She was madly in love with Sam. But Sam's reluctance to leave a very bad situation in order to live with her, eventually tore them apart. Elise left Sam and fell in love with someone else. When he learned of her marriage, Sam was devastated. The birth of her two children seemed to be the final barrier to any happiness they might have had together.

Elise soon realized that the man she married, although a wonderful person, was more of a friend than a husband. She was miserable in a relationship without passion and deep love. Amazingly, she and Sam ran into each other quite coincidentally. They discovered that the magnetic pull between them hadn't abated at all with time. They gravitated back into a relationship that was so passionate and loving, the rest of their lives seemed colorless in comparison. Elise separated from her husband and moved to an area where she could devote herself to the development of her inner, spiritual growth. Although she resisted drifting back into an affair with Sam, he was deeply embedded in her heart and consciousness.

When Sam was presented with the living proof of Elise's devotion to him, although now expressed only on a spiritual plane, his choice of happiness became very clear . . . absolutely black and white. Even so, it took quite a long time for Sam to break the shackles that seemed to bind him to a wife who verbally abused him and was coldly uninterested in anything he might say or do. Not only was his health being threatened, but his sense of self was being seriously damaged. He himself couldn't understand why he would stick around to be punched like a wounded dog hemmed in by a pack of wolves. The closeness he felt for his daughters was a strong detriment to ending his marriage, but as the girls grew older, Sam could see that they were being harmed by the atmosphere pervading their home life.

Sam and Elise finally came together again and made some hard, conscious choices of a lifestyle they could both accept. They found apartments near each other in the city so that they could create separate homes for their children but could be together as much as possible. The arrangement worked for a while, but this was not an ideal solution for Elise, who wanted to be with the man she loved on a more permanent basis. Sam was very hesitant to take the next step and file for a divorce. Elise found herself in a similar situation as when she first met Sam, although the relationship was now on a more honest level. Sam's wife still held the upper hand, however, and constantly intruded on their lives.

A deep kind of sadness lay as a foundation to Elise's newfound happiness. Since she and Sam have a wonderful, sincere ability to talk about everything, it was no surprise to Sam that Elise wanted him to end his marriage and make a real commitment to her. Neither Elise nor Sam could understand why he was so bound to a woman he disliked intensely. Sam admitted to himself that he had never really loved her in the first place. So why couldn't he walk away, in relief, to a woman who obviously made him so happy? Sam told himself that, although he certainly knew he had done everything possible to please his wife and to try to make her happy, it was his sense of responsibility that made him stay in a very destructive relationship. Elise suggested that both she and Sam undergo a regression session to see what might lie behind the complicated emotional situation.

Elise decided to come for her regression session first. After we reviewed her present lifetime, and I suggested that Elise go to a past life, her face took on an incadescent glow. She had a slight smile on her face, and it was clear to me that she was seeing something that made her very happy. I asked her what she was seeing, and she eagerly began to describe a scene to me. She said, "I see myself in a very luxurious setting. It seems to be in the countryside, perhaps England. Evidently I live in a beautiful house. I can see myself dressed in beautiful clothes riding in a carriage." I asked Elise to describe the house, and she said, "It's very grand and absolutely beautiful." I asked her what she did during the day. She replied, "Well, I think I paint. I have two children, a boy and a girl, and lots of help. I seem to go into town periodically because my husband has some duties there. I seem to attend public functions from time to time. My husband is like a country squire, or he's involved with community activities . . . maybe even politics of sorts. We're very much in love, and have beautiful children. I think the children are my two children in this lifetime!" The description Elise gave me of her life in the English countryside seemed ideal, so I asked her how old she lived to be in that time. Elise's reply was startling. She said, "I don't think I live to be very old. I think I die in my middle thirties." She began to cry quietly, so I gently asked her to see the cause of her death. She responded, "I think I get sick with some kind of lung disease . . . like tuberculosis, perhaps. Then things change drastically." Elise was visibly moved at what she was seeing in her mind's eye, and began to sob. She said, "I go very quickly, and my poor husband is absolutely devastated. It's to the point that he can't function. We have no time to prepare anything, or to talk about what he will do after I die. He just falls apart, and begins to drink heavily." I asked Elise about her children. She said, "Well, they miss me, of course, but they are well cared for. We have a staff who've known them since birth and love them a lot. Of course they are sad, but it's my husband that suffers the most. I think he does nothing but drink. He lets everything go. He has no interest in anything, so he abandons all of his duties. He loses everything, and eventually becomes completely dissolute. Oh, it is Sam." Elise began to cry to think of the agony of her bereft husband. She said, "Of course it's Sam. I die so quickly he doesn't have a chance to prepare himself. His health suffers so badly from drinking, he doesn't live to be an old man."

After a period of time, to allow Elise a chance to process the information that had come to her mind, I asked her if they had another lifetime together. Elise replied, "I believe so. I'm seeing a time that we were together in a fairly primitive life. We may be Vikings, and Sam has to leave me to go on a ship. I'm not sure if we're married. I think he must leave before we are actually married, and he never comes back. Oh, my goodness! It seems like he leaves me, very suddenly, in one life, and then I suddenly leave him in the next. I don't want this to happen again." Elise had an astonished look on her face and said, "Do you know, I almost got hit by a car today? It was actually a cab, and I had to jump back before he hit me. I have to be careful now."

I suggested to Elise that she imagine herself in the English countryside again, so that she could talk to Sam in the context of that lifetime. She asked, "What should I say to him?" I replied, "Talk to him about what he would do when you're gone. Heal the situation so that he is encouraged to continue leading a productive life. Tell him that the children need him and that you want him to take care of himself so he'll be ready to meet you in a future life. You want him to have a healthy body." Elise asked me, "Will that work?" My response was "Well, you are together again now, and healing can take place on high levels of inspiration and imagination, best of all. Thoughts are powerful things!"

Sam came to see me for his regression session a few days later. Elise told him about her session with me, as she was very anxious to let him know of their past association. I usually suggest that when a couple are planning to see me only a few days apart, the first person to go through the session might resist the temptation to give information to his or her partner. In that way, a kind of "proof" of the images might emerge in the second session. However, Elise felt that she would be withholding something important from Sam if she didn't tell him about her experience. It was no surprise to me, therefore, that Sam's session was focused on his past relationship with his wife, rather than identifying Elise in a past-life situation.

When Sam began to look at his present life, memories of his babyhood began to emerge. He went to a time period he had almost completely blocked out of his conscious memory. He had been told of the events of the first two years of his life, and he knew what had happened, but he had never viewed those years as if he were reliving them again.

Sam almost died at birth. He was very sick for the first two years of his life and, in fact, was hospitalized for the entire time. He was unable to go home, go outside to play, or even be taken for a walk. He had tuberculosis and was almost completely isolated. He was too weak to get out of his crib. Although his mother came to visit him, she couldn't hold him or even get too close to him. Imagine what it might be like to lie completely still for two years. Imagine not knowing when the time of isolation would be over. And then imagine what you would do if you were too weak to play or do anything at all. Sam did the only thing possible. He developed a patient, stoic quality. He learned to just endure.

When Sam focused on that little baby trapped in a crib, I asked him to become a guardian angel for that child and talk to him about his future life. I suggested that Sam find something to say to that tiny child that would give him hope and encouragement. Obviously no one in his life knew how to do that for him. I also suggested that the endurance he developed at that time was appropriate for his recovery, but not so accurate a response later on. When Sam focused on his level of endurance in the face of a terribly difficult time in his marriage, it was similar to the way he felt as a baby . . . that he simply had no choice but to be stoic and endure.

It is amazing that the significant pattern, and the way we make changes in life emerges from taking a look at the way we are born. It is as if a formula is set in motion that describes all future ways of making changes in life. After pinpointing that birth "formula," I then suggest the person look to a past life to see where the seeds of the difficulty started before conscious memory. In the light of Elise's description of Sam's dissipation in a past life with her, his early health problems made a great deal of sense. As Sam was reviewing the circumstances of his early life, he was, of course, not relating the childhood illness to what Elise had revealed. But the sorrow of losing her in an English lifetime obviously followed him into the present time. Imagine how bereaved he must have felt to drown his sorrows in drinking himself to death, so that he even needed additional time in another life, the present one, to heal. Imagine the guilt he might have felt when he thought of what he might have done to save Elise in that life, and imagine how difficult it would be to abandon a wife again. Elise saw that Sam lost everything he had worked for in their life together. Although Sam is not attached, materially, to the things he has worked so hard to attain in the present time, imagine what a penalty he might fear to set in motion if he repeated the same patterns and lost another wife and family in the present time. Sam has a very strong sense of duty, no matter what kind of abuse he might take in return.

So far in our regression session, Sam neglected to see anything that would help him solve his present dilemma. Everything that came to his mind only reinforced how he must be stoic, endure, and continue to honor his responsibility. Sam began to talk about the material security he was able to give his family in the present time. He was in a quandary about his feelings of nonattachment to those possessions yet his inability to walk away from his luxurious home, family, and possessions. As Sam was describing his town house, it was obvious that it was furnished beautifully and equipped with the latest modern devices. Sam began to describe the small garden in the back of the house. He said, "Do you know, my wife never liked that house. She thought there were evil spirits in the house and even called a Catholic priest to do an exorcism. She was told by a psychic that someone had died in that house and was buried in a corner of the garden. It is true that the house brought only unhappiness, not any joy at all."

Suddenly Sam flashed on another past life. He saw himself as a man living in the same city as in present time, and married to the same woman. Suddenly he described the kitchen and was visibly shaken. He said, "My wife is standing there with a gun in her hand. She is very angry and fires the gun, killing me instantly." Sam focused on what he saw and after some exclamations said, "I can't believe it. It is exactly the same house. She killed me in my last lifetime in that very same house. I am buried in the garden of the house." After a short time, I asked Sam what he might have done to anger her. He said, "Nothing. She just hated me and wanted me out of the way." I finally asked him what happened to her after his death. Was she convicted of the crime? Did she go to jail? Was she able to hide the body? Sam said she got away with the crime, but died shortly afterward of natural causes. Needless to say, Sam was in a state of shock when he realized that he was walking in the same shoes once again. Fortunately, his wife confined her anger toward Sam to mere verbal abuse this time around. But Sam could see how truly destructive it was to continue the relationship.

Somehow it was necessary for Sam to forgive her

for her violence toward him, both in the previous life and in the present time. Only in this way, could he progress to a happy time of life. It was clear to me that Sam was still punishing himself for unfounded guilt he felt about letting Elise die in their former life together. Since he was shot in the chest, he could understand the injury to that part of his body which followed him into the present time. He could also see that he feared having true happiness in a marital situation because true love might be too painful. It is easier for Sam to be stoic and endure a negative situation.

Happy news came less than a month later, when both Elise and Sam called to tell me he had finally filed divorce papers. He said the discussions about his settlement of their material possessions were as amiable as possible under the circumstances, but the important factor was that Sam was working toward self-forgiveness for taking abuse so long and for whatever guilt he felt about Elise in the past.

CHAPTER 6

Past-life jealousy and passion; separation in the present.

When I had set up an appointment for Connie to do a regression session, I was as unprepared for what would emerge as was Connie, for she described, in minute detail, a life spent in a very responsible position. However, the significant factor that would emerge from this astounding revelation had to do with an uneasy romantic relationship that has lasted throughout many lifetimes. The thread that ran through all these experiences was intense jealousy. It contaminated not only the beautiful fabric of an extraordinary past life, but continued into the present life. The jealousy Connie felt then and now was not abated and is still a negative emotion that can ruin her health and sense of well-being.

Connie's session with me was booked at the very last minute. She certainly had no time to prepare for what was to emerge. In fact, until I confirmed the historical significance of what she revealed, I'm very sure Connie had no idea of the historical accuracy of what she saw. Later on, it became a fascinating adventure for her to research information about her life in encyclopedias and books. Both she and I were able to fill in correct details that she revealed on a totally subjective level, for Connie saw herself as a *very* important figure in history. Connie was very shocked at the confirmation of some of her strongest, very personal memories. She presumed that some of her activities had never been known by the public, but it seems that little was kept secret at the time of her prominence.

Connie was not the only one to see the exact situation she described. The young man, who is the love of her life, saw the same correct historical details but from his own perspective with no coaching from Connie. Everything dovetailed exactly.

Connie was going through a very difficult time in her life. She came to me because she thought a regression session might help her untangle some of her conflicted emotions. Connie remet her younger cousin, Tim, when he came back to her town to visit. Their instant mutual attraction created a major problem in her life. Connie was very unhappy in her marriage, but with two children to care for, she had never considered a divorce.

A short time after Tim reappeared, they began having an affair. They saw each other surreptitiously, as often as possible, but there were many days when they could not be together. Worse than her conscience was Connie's intense jealousy of Tim. She was very possessive of him. If he should happen to talk to another woman, she felt incredible rage. She did not dare think of what he might be doing, in his spare evenings, when she was at home with her family. Even though he constantly reassured her of his utter devotion and love, she had many sleepless nights. Tim reminded her that if he did not occasionally go on a date it would look very strange. Tim was young, handsome, well built, and had a charming personality. After agonizing over the situation time and again, Connie finally decided that she just couldn't deal with her inner turmoil. She broke off her relationship with Tim. However, her resolve to avoid Tim didn't last longer than a few days. They were both so in love, they couldn't stand to be apart from each other. Their magnetic attraction went far beyond a logical approach to the sticky situation.

Finally, Connie hit upon a solution. She decided to open a restaurant, with Tim as her manager so that they would have a reason to be in each other's company. This plan of action meant that Tim would have to give up his own business. Originally, Tim was reluctant to take such a step. He was a successful photographer and traveled all over the world on assignments. Tim loved his life and his creative challenges. On one hand, he wanted to be with Connie as much as possible, but he had no guarantee that, after such a sacrifice on his part, she would actually leave her husband and be with him. Furthermore, he hated the restaurant business.

The biggest obstacle for Connie in divorcing her husband and marrying Tim was getting family approval. Her father's opinion meant a lot to her, and he would never condone her marrying her cousin.

The fact that Tim was a younger man, taboo in Connie's world, was beside the point. Both Connie and Tim were caught in a tangled web. Connie couldn't understand why she, a sensible lady, couldn't just walk away from the situation. Her guilt, concern for her reputation, and fear of being ostracized by her family could not override her passionate need to be with Tim.

We began Connie's regression session by reviewing events in her life, going backward to childhood and birth. After that, I suggested that Connie give herself an important directive, "I want to go to a past life that will help me understand the circumstances of now."

After only a slight pause she said, "I see myself coming down a long flight of steps. I have on a beautiful gown, really elaborate, with a real high collar and big sleeves. There are a lot of flounces on the skirt. I have lots of jewelry around my neck, and there are jewels on the dress, too. I'm going to some sort of very special occasion, like a coronation."

Suddenly Connie said, "Oh! It's my coronation. I'm going to be queen!" Even though her eyes were closed, I could tell that Connie was seeing something she had not expected. She continued describing the pictures that were forming in her mind's eye. "There is a huge hall, like a banquet hall, with a huge table. There are tapestries and chandeliers. Everything is heavy and wood-carved . . . massive . . . the chairs at the table look so big, they are almost too big."

Part of my technique in conducting regression sessions without using hypnosis is to ask seemingly unimportant questions. This allows my client to focus on details, using the left brain, while the right brain has a chance to come up with the real issues. I asked Connie a simple question, "Are your mother and father there?" She replied, "No, they're both dead. My little brother has just died. He wasn't a baby, but he wasn't grown up, either." I continued my line of questioning by asking what country this might be. She didn't hesitate before she said, "England." I asked her name, and she said, "Anne."

It was easy to work with Connie. It was hardly necessary to ask her questions, as her impressions poured out. She seemed to be looking at a film that was being projected in her mind. When someone can see, or sense, things so vividly I am usually able to tune in with them. In Connie's case, I felt I was walking down the stairs with her, seeing the scene before her as vividly as was she. The thought that ran through my mind when she said "Anne" was very distinct. I said to myself, "She's Elizabeth, not Anne," and I felt chills run down the back of my neck and spine.

An avid student of the Elizabethan period of history, I was sure Connie was talking about the coronation of Elizabeth I of England. I could almost see the gown she was wearing, especially when she described the big, high collar. I knew that Elizabeth was crowned queen upon the death of her sister Mary, and that Mary's coronation took place after the early demise of their brother, young King Edward. I was sure Connie was unaware of the historical significance of what she was saying, and didn't know who she was talking about. It was interesting to me that she didn't mention Mary's reign at all.

Mary and Elizabeth had never been easy in each other's company. That was partly because of the enmity between their mothers, and partly because of their religious differences. Elizabeth had been very close to her younger brother, whereas Edward was ill at ease with Mary because she was such a staunch Catholic. Edward and Elizabeth wholeheartedly embraced Protestantism.

Mary could never forget that Elizabeth's mother, Anne Boleyn, had usurped her own mother's place as queen. Anne Boleyn had caused Mary great misery when she was young. When she was queen, Mary kept Elizabeth under close guard for most of her reign, even confining her to the Tower of London for a while. The moment Mary died, Elizabeth wiped out all thoughts of Mary. She even ignored her duty as the executor of Mary's will and overlooked Mary's last requests. She had chafed under the unreasonable restrictions the former queen had imposed on her and could not forget the death threats. While Mary was still alive, there were many rumors of plans to oust Mary and put Elizabeth on the throne instead. Although Mary could never prove any involvement on Elizabeth's part, she imprisoned her in the Tower and threatened to take Elizabeth's life as a traitor. It was not an easy crown that lay on Elizabeth's head.

As we continued, Connie identified her father in this life as her adviser when she was queen. She described the restriction she felt around him in the former life and said it was the same in the present time. As if to confirm the truth of this painful realization, Connie burst into tears at what she was seeing. Then I asked her how the English people react toward her. She replied, "They think I am wonderful because everything I do is for the people. I don't seem to be doing anything for myself. Every decision I make is what's best for the people. I try to do things for people who are poor, because my father seemed to be more concerned about himself than the people. I am more concerned about the country. He was more egotistical and wanted fine things for himself. I have to sacrifice myself because all the people are depending on me. It seems I feel he didn't really do what was right and I am going to do what is right, come hell or high water." Of course Queen Elizabeth's description of Henry VIII, although understated, was very accurate.

"I have a strong sense of moral obligation. I am in a constant battle with myself because I'm not able to do anything as far as my personal life is concerned. Everything has to be hidden." Connie began to cry, afresh, at that realization. Suddenly she began crying quite hard, and I asked her what she was seeing. She said, "I'm looking in the corner where there is a doorway." Her tears prevented her from saying any more for quite a while. At long last she said, "It's Tim."

When I felt she was ready to go on, I asked, "Why are you crying?" She replied, "Because I can't have him." I asked her to explain that, and she continued, "For one thing, he's married, but the real reason is they won't let me. It's not right for the country. It wouldn't be good for the kingdom or the people. He's not the right person." I asked if she was ever able to marry him, and she said, "No, I have to be very careful not to let my adviser know how I feel about him. Everything I do in the relationship has to be sneaky. We can't just say anything to each other, and we can't go anywhere together. He has to appear to be just a friend." The tears started flowing again, and it was obvious that the emotion she was feeling was very deep. She said, "It's just the same thing all over again. Everything has to be whitewashed."

After more specific questions about the situation then, she continued, "My adviser won't let me marry him or even see him. He keeps telling me it will cause trouble. He (Tim) is around me all the time at the court. It's like I just have to have him with me. He is supposed to have a function at the court, but I actually create a job for him and give him a title as well, I think. I have to have a good reason for him to be here. There are always men around trying to persuade me to marry them. There are so many people bringing me gifts, trying to do things for me, and he is one of my suitors.

"I think his family is a bit dishonest, which makes it even more difficult. He's not royalty, either. But the first time I see him, it's like the feeling of meeting a long-lost friend. It is a complete and total communication and feeling of comfort. I don't have to pretend anything with him. I can just be myself. He uplifts my spirit and makes me feel good about everything, making sure that all is smooth for me. He is around me for a few years, and then he is married. He is really impatient because I won't do anything about our love. I am supposed to be a virgin, but we are having a relationship that no one knows about. I have a maid who helps us go away together. We go for rides in the country and really have fun. She covers for us." I asked how she found out about the marriage, and she replied, "Someone tells me. He is afraid to tell me himself, but a man who is watching everything he does is really eager to tell me the news. He says in effect, 'Now, you can just forget about him.' I am so upset ... I get really mad and banish him from the country. I say, 'Now you've done it. Now you'll have to pay for it.' Everyone is trying to get me married. They keep telling me to get serious about someone. They keep picking people they think will be good for the country. I pretend to enjoy the whirlwind that starts, but am really thinking about my love. I had given him a ring, but I take that right away from him when he gets married. He didn't know that I'd react so violently or that I'd banish him from my sight. It's just too painful to have him right there in front of me when I can't have him. I can never let anyone know how I feel. I have to be really hypocritical, because if I don't do everything just right, there is someone else to take my place."

I asked Connie to tell me about the other person. It had become increasingly obvious to me that Connie was unaware of the details of her description from an historical point of view. She was recounting everything from a deeply personal and emotional perspective, yet her observations were historically accurate. I deliberately avoided leading her to what I knew to be correct. Connie said, "It is another woman. She isn't well. She isn't as much in control as I am and does not have a strong constitution. She is really emotional. She is always putting pressure on me because she has children and I'm not even married. I think I make her physically sick through my mental power." I asked her the name of the other person, and she replied, "Mary." Connie gave a very accurate description of Mary Queen of Scots.

She continued telling me what came to her. "I think I had him put in prison. He wasn't married very long. He didn't want to be married to her, so he got her out of the way so he could come back to me. I wanted to lock him up so he couldn't be with her, but I really didn't have a good reason. After he kills his wife, I have to lock him up, even though I'm glad he has done it. It doesn't look good if I don't punish him for the crime. Even though it is painful to put him in prison, I know he understands that it's what I have to do. Later I pardon him. He gets sick and pleads with me to let him out of prison. Other people say I can't do that. I am skirting dangerous ground with that one. They're ready to pounce on me anyway because I'm not married."

Emotion overcame Connie once more. She described his death. She told me that she was dying inside but did not dare show any grief at all. She concluded her story by skimming over the rest of her life as a lonely woman with a tremendous sense of responsibility and pressure from the outside world.

After the regression session, Connie told me how tired she was. Finally she said, "When you asked me my name, there were two names that popped into my head. I said Anne, but I think I was Elizabeth, and my mother was Anne." I told Connie a little of the historical data about that period of time and assured her that what she recounted was historically accurate. The hour was quite late, and we were both overly tired. We decided to meet at a local library the next day in order to confirm the details of her story. We also made an agreement not to tell Tim any of the details of her regression. We hoped he would be willing to do his own regression session, and we didn't want to prejudice him in any way. If he also recounted the events of that time, we'd have an interesting corroboration of her memory.

The next day we met like conspirators to pore over the encyclopedia. As she read, Connie had an expression of pure amazement on her face. "Look at this," she said, and pointed to a paragraph about the Earl of Leicester, the love of Queen Elizabeth's life. It said that his real name was Robert Dudley. Since I knew that already, I didn't see the significance of her astonishment. She finally said, "Don't you know Tim's last name? It's Dudley!"

Subsequently, I did a regression with Tim. As we had agreed, Connie had deliberately kept the details of her session a secret. I was not at all sure that Tim would recall anything that remotely resembled her story. I have never tried to prove anything about reincarnation, nor do I worry about whether the information an individual reveals to himself is real. I'm interested in the healing effects in the present life that can come as a result of new awareness. If the information is real, or merely a metaphor, the important factor is the impact it can have on present-day problems. However, if Tim should *happen* to see the same situation in his regression session, it would be very significant for both Tim and Connie.

Tim was a willing subject, even though Connie had rather insisted that he do a regression session. As he reviewed some painful moments in his childhood, he said he felt like a stranger among strangers. I could tell from Tim's astrological chart that he didn't feel he belonged to his family. He described a situation in his early life that led to a decision not to trust anyone, ever again. He had learned how to shut off his feelings. Tim was not a man to show emotion.

Although Tim's eyes were closed, tears began to well up, sliding down his cheeks. Then he began to shiver. I asked him to tell me what he was feeling. He didn't answer and, once again, I asked him to talk to me and share what he was thinking. Finally he said, "I'm so cold." Assuming he was talking about the air-conditioning in the room, I turned it off and put a jacket around his shoulders. He said, "It's another life. I'm just so cold."

Tim said he was wearing a bathing suit. I asked what country he was in, and he replied, "Denmark comes to mind. It's cold, really cold." I asked if he was in a swimming pool, and he replied, "A lake." Tim continued, "I'm swimming by myself. There's a dock somewhere. I have a mustache, and I'm heavier than I am now, but about the same height." I asked if this was where he lived. He shook his head, no. I stopped to ask if he wanted me to put a blanket around him, and he said, "Yes." Later on, Tim commented that it didn't help at all because the cold was from the inside.

Tim was in such obvious discomfort, I knew he was experiencing a deeply emotional reaction. He asked if we could stop the session, but I assured him it was necessary to go on. I couldn't leave him in the middle of a bad memory. Finally I asked him to describe the scene before him. He continued, "I'm looking up through the water. I can see through it, but it is as if I'm under the surface. I'm alive, but I can't straighten out, and I can't get to the surface. My stomach really hurts. I've been trying to figure out why my stomach hurts so much." Tim was bent over, shivering, and rocking while clutching himself around the waist. I wanted to alleviate his discomfort, but I knew I had to continue. The pain was obviously a reaction from a past life. "There are three people standing above me. There's a lady in a big, big dress. It's big at the bottom, straight at the top, with a big collar. There's a man with her. Someone is standing and someone is sitting down." After a slight pause, he said, "I'm not sure I'm in water at all. It's like I'm seeing them through glass. They're just looking at me. It's like they're standing there waiting for me to die."

With that awareness, a fresh batch of tears poured down his face. He was clearly hurting on more than a physical level. I asked him to describe his station in life. He replied, "I'm rich, very rich. I'm noble. I'm part of them. We don't have to do anything, we're so rich." Then he came back to the emotion he was feeling so strongly. "I'm shocked that they're my friends, and they're not doing anything to help me." I asked if he recognized either of the people from this lifetime, and Tim replied, "I feel like I know them. I don't like the man standing there, but she's someone I love." I asked again if he recognized her from this life, and he began sobbing. He said, "It can't be, it can't be . . ." It was clear that he was seeing Connie. As a last question I asked, "What country are you from?" He didn't hesitate. "England," he replied.

It seemed appropriate to stop our work at this point. As Tim opened his eyes, he said, "I want to see Connie." In anticipation of what Tim might be feeling about that moment of seeming abandonment Connie was close by, waiting for him to finish his session. As they clung together, there was no need for Connie to ask him what he had recalled. I quietly slipped out of the room.

In retrospect, Tim's experience of severe stomach

pains was amazing. The Earl of Leicester had died of stomach cancer. Although Tim's recollections and descriptions did not emerge the same way as Connie's, I felt sure he was recalling the same events, but from his perspective. The details of the last days of the Earl of Leicester were somewhat mixed in Tim's retelling, but the gist of the story was accurate. His accompanying emotions could not have been less than true.

As a student of history, I was excited to locate reference books so that I could review the events of Elizabeth and Leicester's lives. I was quite sure neither Connie nor Tim had ever done any research into the events of that time period. I found two books in particular, *The First Elizabeth*, by Carolly Erickson and *Sir Francis Bacon*, by Jean Overton Fuller, that confirmed the accounts given by both Connie and Tim in their regression sessions. Reprints of those sections that are most relevant to their descriptions can be found in my book *Astrology and Your Past Lives*. I was truly astounded at the accuracy of Connie's and Tim's memory when I read the historical accounts.

Shortly after Drake's great victory at sea, Leicester and the queen dined together. Leicester mentioned his health, and Elizabeth suggested he should take the baths at Buxton. On his way to the spa on September 7, 1588, her birthday, he died. Although Tim saw himself in the water with terrible stomach cramps, I could make a leap of faith and realize that Tim mistook the water for his intention to take the baths or suspect that he had been swimming prior to his decision to go to Buxton.

Connie's description of the coronation dress with "jewels on the dress, too" was quite accurate. Elizabeth had a mania for jewels. Her perspective about her relationship with Dudley, later Earl of Leicester, was interesting. In the regression session, Connie presumed they had fooled everyone into thinking they were just friends. In the literary description, it seemed everyone knew they were having an affair. In fact, the rumor of the time was that Sir Francis Bacon was actually a child of Elizabeth and Leicester.

The historical account of the death of Leicester's wife, Amy, was somewhat different from the harsher account revealed by Connie in her session. The sequence of events was also somewhat out of order in Connie's account, for Leicester was suspected of killing his first wife, Amy Robsart, but it was his later marriage to Lettice Knollys, after he had given up any hope of a marriage to Elizabeth, that so infuriated her. Not only was Elizabeth hurt by his disloyalty, but her vanity was wounded. Evidently they quarreled openly, in front of the whole court. Leicester and Lettice were secretly married sometime after Lettice's husband died in 1576. The discovery of the marriage both shocked and enraged the queen. She ordered him seized and shut up in an isolated tower in Greenwich park before his imprisonment in the Tower of London.

After Leicester had spent the week in involuntary isolation, Elizabeth thought better of her first reaction. She let it be known that he had merely been shut away to take medicine. Although he left the court to stay at one of his own houses, he was clearly in the doghouse, and had forfeited a measure of a special bond that had existed between them. Leicester was afraid that with a loss of power, he might also lose his wealth. He must have felt like a loving pet that was suddenly ignored by his master.

Perhaps the most astounding fact that emerged was Connie's casual account of Leicester's killing of his first wife, Amy Robsart. The court was in such an uproar over the scandal that a demand was made for a formal investigation into the charges. The gossip of the day was that the queen was so in love with Lord Robert that she was only waiting for Amy to die in order to marry him. Amy was ill with what modern medicine might have diagnosed as terminal cancer. Amy had been found dead at the foot of a staircase, after sending the servants out for the day. Leicester himself demanded there should be an inquest. It was shown he had not been at Cumnor, where she died, and a verdict of accidental death was recorded. The breast cancer had spread into the neck, causing spontaneous fracture of the spine when she fell. Reports reached the court that Mary Queen of Scots, Elizabeth's mortal enemy, had said, "The Queen of England is going to marry her horsekeeper, who has killed his wife to make room for her." For Elizabeth to have married Leicester in these circumstances would have further fed the scandal. From being seen everywhere with him, now she was hardly seen at all. She withdrew into herself, in Whitehall Palace, for the winter.

The jealousy and intrigues between Elizabeth and Leicester lasted throughout their lives. The rumor was that Elizabeth was pregnant with Leicester's child and that during the time she was isolated after the death of Leicester's wife, she could have been carrying the child, later to be adopted and named Francis Bacon. She had confessed to the Bishop de Quadra that she was not without some sin. The bishop thought she meant she was not a virgin.

There were many rumors of a secret marriage, but evidently such a ceremony never took place. A report in Stowe's *Historical Memoranda* gives an account of a proposed quiet wedding set for April 12, 1566. "She was late, and he gave up waiting. In fact, she had set out with two of her ladies-in-waiting, but he met her on the way, and they simply rode back to Greenwich Place. The queen had not gone through with it again. With such frustrations, it is said that there was further withdrawal on Leicester's part after this." Connie's description of the first time she met Tim was confirmed, "The first time I see him it's like the feeling of a long-lost friend." Elizabeth and Leicester met as eight-year-olds, when they were both confined to the Tower of London. They had a special empathy between them even then, according to Erickson. "Though Elizabeth was not a confiding child, she confided in him." Connie's description of his family: "I think his family was a bit dishonest. They're not quiet on the up and up, which makes it even more difficult" was a mild understatement. Leicester's father had been the adviser to Elizabeth's brother, King Edward, and had eventually been tried as a traitor and found guilty. Among other things, he had concealed the death of the young king for as much time as possible, in order to set Lady Jane Grey on the throne. Mary was Henry VIII's true heir, according to his will. Jane only ruled as queen for a very short time, until the elder Dudley could be ousted. (Mary was duly crowned, and John Dudley was decapitated, drawn, and quartered. Parts of his body were displayed all over London.)

I saw Connie about six months after her regression session, and I asked her to describe the changes or benefits that may have come as a result of the sessions. Connie replied, "The first thing I noticed, immediately after the regression, was that I no longer felt like I had to live my life according to what someone else expected of me. That in itself has been tremendously important. I have also had a lot of déjà vu, especially between Tim and me. We would be laughing and just having fun, and I would get flashbacks." Tim volunteered, "One thing I have never understood about our relationship is my attachment to Connie. I understand the emotional part, but I would rather do something for Connie than take care of my own business. For instance, I can't stand the restaurant business, yet I'm there working very hard. After a few months, I was ready to leave. I hate the hours, the pettiness, but I just can't leave her. I know what she's going through and what she has to deal with. I try to persuade her to sell the restaurant and leave this town, as we have no social freedom here. Yet I continue to stay somewhere I don't like, just to be with her. It's such a contrast from my past. Nobody could ever tie me down before."

Connie continued to have spontaneous recollections of other lives when she and Tim were together. These lifetimes were not grand, but very simple. The subsequent memories seemed to occur after the grandeur of the English court. It is probable that Connie as Elizabeth made an unconscious decision to do away with splendor in favor of love. However, the pain and jealousy inherent in their relationship was still there. Connie said, "We were living in this country two different times. I saw myself in a print housedress and an apron. He had on pants with suspenders. I was somewhere close to the beach, probably the East Coast. He left me then . . . on horseback. He left me for someone else then, too. I saw myself very upset. I had children, and I felt really abandoned. The other life was really beautiful. It was a tropical, gorgeous, lush environment. We were artists together, living in some heavenly paradise. We were very successful then." Tim is an exceptionally talented artist in this life as well.

The lifetime of devotion and caring between Connie and Tim may have come earlier than the English lifetime. Connie did not describe what may have led to her birth into a rulership position other than to briefly describe the success of a simple but productive life. The jealousy had not yet entered into their relationship, it seems, until Connie as queen was not able to have the man she loved by her side.

About a year after our first meeting, Connie called me and said, "Something has happened that is so personal I can't tell anyone but you and Tim." She was reluctant to reveal any more on the telephone, but promised to go into more detail when we saw each other next. When we were together, she said, "One morning I woke up and remembered a dream I had that night. I was sitting at this enormous desk, just huge, and I was writing with a feather pen in a script that was different. I was very dressed up in a big dress with a high collar and big sleeves, and I was writing a poem. I could see some of the words, but I couldn't remember it. I had to get up, as I had pressing appointments, but a few days later, I decided I would meditate and try to remember that poem.

"I lay down and went into a real deep state of meditation. I visualized the desk and the chair, and I started to 'read it' off the page. I'd see some part of it, then jump up and write it down. Then I'd forget, go back, and lie down to see some more lines. I could see some lines very clearly, but then it would skip and go on to the next verse. Three or four lines would be very clear in one verse, but only a couple in another. It was an extremely personal experience.

"The only thing I could think of that day was to find out if that poem exists. I went to the library and found a reference book that is an index for poetry. The poems are listed three ways: by title, first line, and author's name. I had seen the title as 'On Monsieur's Departure,' so I looked first under titles in the reference book. I was a bit disappointed when it wasn't there. Then I decided to look under the first line. I wasn't sure that I had remembered the first line, but I thought I had been able to see the top of the page in my meditation. I decided I wasn't going to go to the author first, just on principle. I wanted to find that first line and then see who wrote it. It might have been by someone else.

"As I was turning the pages, my hands were just shaking. I was going down the list and . . . my God . . . there it was . . . the first line of the poem. The author was Queen Elizabeth. I was shaking so hard, I had to sit down. I was just stunned. When Tim arrived, we tried to find a book in the library that contained the whole poem. We discovered that there was only one book that contained that poem. The book was so rare, it was in the rare-book section of a university library in a nearby city. I was so shaken, I couldn't go there, so Tim went to find the book. When he arrived at the university, he discovered that he needed permission even to see the book. It took a few days to get that permission, but when he did, he went back and was able to copy the poem word for word."

Connie reluctantly showed me the two pieces of paper. One piece of paper was written in her own handwriting with several lines unevenly spaced. The spaces between certain lines indicated that the lines were not consecutive. Connie explained the reason she felt the poem had not been titled in the rare book. "Evidently I didn't give the poem a title because that would have given away my feelings. I wrote the poem after the Earl of Leicester had died. Since I couldn't show my grief at the news of his death, I spent a day by myself and poured out my feeling on paper."

There seemed to be no way that Connie could have stumbled on the poem by accident in her school days. There is always a possibility of an individual's ability to tap into a universal stream of consciousness, or the Akashic Records, as they are known, yet that is quite a feat in itself. These lines seemed to be etched into Connie's subconscious mind. The lines Connie remembered were:

> I grieve, and dare not show my discontent;
> I love, and yet am forced to seem to hate;
> This too familiar care does make me rue it;
> Oh, be more cruel, Love, and so be kind;
> Let me float or sink, be high or low;

Those five lines were exactly five of the lines found scattered throughout the entire poem. (See my book *Astrology and Your Past Lives*, Simon and Schuster, 1987, for the reprint of the entire poem.)

It is obvious that Tim and Connie have a deep, abiding love for each other. They have had many lives together to resolve the relationship that was established centuries ago. If Connie were to focus on the very beginning of their association, she might find the roots of their love and be able to go past the blocks that prevent her from trusting and committing herself to Tim. Connie has confessed that her greatest fear about him is his attraction to other women. Evidently she was very jealous and possessive of him in Elizabethan times, even though he proved his devotion to her countless times. She has another memory of a lifetime in which Tim abandoned her and their children. Those scars can be very deep. She is sure his attention to others is only an ego gratification for him and has nothing to do with a lack of love for her, but she hesitates to trust him completely. She is always afraid Tim will leave her again.

After the discovery of the poem written by Queen Elizabeth to Leicester, both Connie and Tim have an entirely different perspective on their situation. For one thing, Connie no longer feels her life revolves around her restaurant. She has decided to continue its operation as long as it is productive, but she has rediscovered an executive ability that can be channeled in many directions. After the memory of the lifetime spent together as artists, where they were very successful, new ideas have come to mind about work they can do together. They have decided to focus on promotion of artistic, creative products.

Tim and Connie are not the only people who have intrigue and jealousies that need to be resolved. When an attraction is strong or a dislike is intense, some kind of past association has occurred to create such a reaction. It is not important for Tim and Connie to live in the memory of the Elizabethan era, yet going back to that time we can help them rewrite their script.

What emerged from the regression sessions can give Connie and Tim tremendous insight about their present-day association. In Elizabethan England, there were many problems that kept them from being together. However, it was really Connie's fears that prevented her from marrying her lifelong love. History might have been quite different if Queen Elizabeth had followed her heart and married the Earl of Leicester. If Elizabeth, in the face of her duty, had decided she was unable to marry him but had nobly wished him personal happiness, the pattern of the next life may have changed drastically. No doubt Connie's husband in the American life had a subconscious need to pay her back for the pain she caused him when he was the Earl of Leicester and she was Elizabeth. In the present lifetime, Connie and Tim may not be able to be together again, but it is important to focus on the here and now of their relationship.

Tim had taken giant steps to express his love for Connie in the present and to constantly reassure her by demonstrating his continuing support of her life choices. The high drama and public awareness of their private lives have de-escalated somewhat in the present, but it seems as if they have chosen circumstances, once again, that are obstacles to their marriage. Connie and Tim can be assured that they will always be together in some kind of loving association, even if marriage is not possible. And, it is important to set up conditions of future lives together by the decisions they make now.

Healing the past, by consciously and deliberately

forgiving each other, can pave the way for greater joy and happiness between Connie and Tim. That kind of healing is almost automatic when a past-life regression takes place. But in order to truly forgive a person or situation, it is necessary to know exactly what one is forgiving.

Tim and Connie can take their mutual experience a step further to release greater creativity and energy between them. If they could use their past-life experience as a metaphor, it is possible to imagine what they might have accomplished if they were working together for the welfare of the country. They might have worked hard to institute land reform, or bring about better legal procedures. Perhaps they might have looked at the economic situation that occurred as a result of land revocation, or inaugurated new levels of education for the poor. Only Tim and Connie know what projects might have been dear to their hearts. Those same ideas can be patterns for activities they might choose in the present time.

Connie mentioned that, as a result of seeing themselves as artists in a later time frame, they have decided to become more involved in artistic projects. A closer look at Elizabethan England could be productive as a stimulus for important activities now. They may not have needed a marriage to work together on projects that might have benefited mankind.

Connie has mentioned that she avoids ambitious projects that might bring her recognition and acclaim because the pressures were too hard in the past. Her personal life is more important to her in this lifetime.

Yet leadership qualities are part of her inner nature. How could a cooperative association between Connie and Tim bring out the best qualities of leadership in each of them now? What facets of their personalities could be strengthened by their mutual concern for each other and for mankind? Perhaps the most important of all is to realize that the strength they possess in their continued love for each other can heal past jealousies and negative karma by the dynamic and positive qualities of a more universal love. That decision to make a contribution can be used not only for enrichment of their own and others' lives, but on a broader scale.

In the final analysis, love is the greatest healing agent of all, but pure love is unselfish. The desire for the best in the life of the partner, even if self-sacrifice is necessary now, allows love to exist on a cosmic level. Hopefully that love can be experienced in a future life in the most positive, wonderful way.

CHAPTER 7

Past-life debts or obligation; financial conditions now.

On the surface, life can seem terribly unfair. One of the areas that has created the most dissension on a worldwide, political level relates to the "haves" and the "have nots." A terrible period of history began at the times of the French and, later, the Russian Revolutions. Brutality was rampant against the groups of people who seemingly had everything and ignored the plight of the poor. The issues related to poverty and opulent wealth exist on all levels of society even though we, in the United States, live in a democratic society. A sometimes sad fact is that in the light of reincarnation, everything is fair and just and ultimately democratic.

Each human being really does have a chance to rise to whatever heights their imagination can take them. From a higher, cosmic point of view, we are all equal, but on an earth level jealousies, resentment, and anger over material issues can lead to violent crimes. Why do some people have the great good fortune to live with no financial worries, whereas some people seem destined to scrape out a bare living? It is tragic to realize that there are still people all over the world who are starving. Will we ever be able to bring these injustices into the cosmic light of abundance? Hopefully in the new century, as we enter the true Aquarian age, more information about our own karmic debts will help heal wrongful ideas about wealth. New concepts of material security can enable mankind to have what is supposedly their due.

Some interesting information about material well-being emerged in the book *Dweller on Two Planets*. This book was dictated by the spirit Phylos to a young man who had no idea what he was writing. In fact, the material was dictated backward, so it made no sense at all to the writer. He was told to burn a section of the book, and he dutifully followed orders. He was also instructed to register the date of completion and put the manuscript into a vault until a certain time period. When the book was published, the spirit Phylos had predicted certain inventions that would come into being; such as electricity, the telegraph, and other conveniences we are now quite accustomed to.

According to Phylos, there was a group of people living near the area we now know as Egypt, although this was during the epoch of Atlantis, who had the true gift of manifestation. These people were able to sit at a bare table, as an example, wave an imaginary magic wand, and produce food and drink of their choice. There was no need to work for a living, nor till the soil for food. It was a natural gift inherent in their spiritual natures. However, according to Phylos, the king of the nation was very perturbed over the spiritual decline of the people. They seemed to forget that this gift was connected to their highest natures. When they neglected their spiritual values, and took this gift for granted, the ability to manifest was taken away from them. No longer able to use the mind to create what was needed, they had to work for their survival and existence. Ever after that time, man has been forced to deal with the material world in a new way.

In psychological terms, patterns of childhood can have a lot to do with financial conditions. One young lady confessed that during her childhood, her mother repeatedly said, "I have champagne tastes, but a beer pocketbook." This young lady appears to have the same consciousness about her material well-being. As an astrologer, I've often been asked about children born at exactly the same time at the same place, who apparently have very different lives. My classic example is that two children have Saturn, a planet that can describe restriction or worry, in their second house of finance. I suggest that one child is born to a poor family whereas the other child is born to a wealthy family. Both children will have strong considerations about money. The wealthy child may worry and put additional stress on himself to preserve the family fortune, whereas the poor child will be determined to build a family fortune. So it follows that a person with great wealth in his or her background may have a wealthy consciousness or feel poor no matter the size of his bank account. The opposite can be true. An individual with a poverty-stricken background may grow up to build a gigantic financial empire.

We may have to look to see what lies on the thread of consciousness to know what kind of underlying patterns exist in regard to financial well-being. In many instances during a regression session, it becomes clear that financial consciousness can be connected not only to past lives, but past-life relationships.

In one instance, Lucinda flashed to a lifetime in Germany. She thought she might be able to resolve a deep wound that was connected to the death of her mother when she was a teenager. Although Lucinda is now in her twenties, she is still in great pain over that loss, and has never been able to understand why her adored mother was taken away from her at such a tender age. To her great surprise, Lucinda saw that a similar loss had occurred in a German lifetime. Her mother had died of an illness, leaving Lucinda as a poverty-stricken young girl. Lucinda placed that life around the 1800s in a small Germanic city. Lucinda was left alone with no one to care for her. She might have been able to find shelter in a church and become a nun, as happened many times with destitute young women in those early times, but Lucinda chose to become a prostitute on the streets of that city. She was lucky enough to attract a wealthy clientele and recognized one young man from her present life. It was ironic and amusing to see that Karl was a client from that lifetime, who had just entered her present life very briefly. She knew that Karl had been a prominent man in German society, and treated her like a woman he might have wanted to marry . . . not like a prostitute at all. Lucinda felt that he might have made some kind of financial settlement with her to help her leave the ranks of the street ladies of the time. She realized she didn't remain a prostitute all her life. Karl was due to have an appointment with me for his own regression session just a few days later.

Lucinda discovered that a lot of her fears, concerning her present-day precarious financial situation, stemmed from that lifetime. Lucinda was studying acting, and did various modeling and acting jobs, including some commercials, to pay her bills. But, as many young actresses, Lucinda was always on a financial edge. Some of the trade shows she did and some of the modeling jobs were not up to the standards of acting that she dreamed about, but she said, "At least I don't have to be a waitress. I can pay my bills, and I would never do something sleazy. The revelation of this lifetime helps me understand a concern that has really plagued me. Whenever I go on an audition, I worry that I'm prostituting myself! I don't know of another actress who feels that way. After all, I'm earning an honest living with an eye to more challenging roles in the future. I'm a dedicated actress and have high hopes of graduating to film and television. But if I'm up for something and have to smile and be charming when I don't feel that way,

I worry that I'm going against my principles. Then I mentally shake myself and remind myself that I'm lucky not to have to do menial jobs to get by. Now that feeling is very clear to me in light of a past life." A deeper comprehension of her choice of prostitution instead of a spiritual life lay in her combined pain and anger over her mother's death. She saw quite clearly, that her decision was born of a thought directed to her dead mother, "See what you've made me do! Aren't you ashamed of me now?" Then the sadness emerged when she realized that attitude was her only way of dealing with the devastating blow of her loss. Lucinda was astounded at what she had revealed to herself, and was sure that a block to future success in the theater had been lifted. She no longer had to punish herself for a decision she'd made almost one hundred and fifty years ago.

Since Karl was visiting the United Sates from his native Germany, Lucinda didn't foresee any future relationship with him other than a momentary, wonderful, loving, romantic liaison. Karl and Lucinda met quite by accident, and Lucinda invited him to stay with her in her apartment during his short visit. They both felt a deep bond of love and friendship and soon drifted into a sexual relationship. The mutual attraction was very strong. When Lucinda thought about Karl leaving her to go back to Germany, she became very sad. Because of her dedication to her career and the job Karl had undertaken in his native country, a future relationship did not seem part of the equation.

Karl was born into a successful banking family and was on vacation during a break in his internship at a German hospital. He had completed his basic training as a physician, and was specializing in psychiatry. He confessed to Lucinda that he found it very rough going. His work placed him in a locked psychiatric ward in a hospital. He was afraid, at times, that he might identify too much with the patients, and he had real fears of becoming insane himself. After experiencing a regression session with me, when she picked up on the German lifetime and recognized Karl, she suggested that he see me, too. She was curious to know if he would recognize her from the life as a prostitute.

Karl reviewed his early life and childhood, going in reverse order, and revealed an amazingly loving family. His mother and father doted on their only son and were very proud of his accomplishments in medical school. Nevertheless, Karl recognized a tendency to be very hard on himself and knew he had to maintain a tight control over his sensitive feelings. He knew he had to accomplish something in his life. He couldn't afford to relax and enjoy a comfortable life as a banker's son.

Karl had an opportunity to travel during school breaks, and had become very well acquainted with architecture that had been built during 1835 and 1848. Karl had been intrigued by the life of Emperor Friederich Wilhelm IV, who reigned only a short thirteen years in Austria. Friederich's death was still a mystery to historians. It was never known exactly how he died, because he had been declared insane after suffering two paralytic strokes, and was succeeded by his brother, Wilhelm I, who was named regent. During his reign, Friederich Wilhelm IV had spent most of his time designing beautiful castles and buildings throughout Austria. Karl visited every single site with great interest. It was a known fact that Friederich was considered to be insane, yet his artistic accomplishments were extraordinary. Suddenly, as we were reviewing a past life, Karl recognized himself as Freiderich IV. He was in absolute shock over that revelation. He saw his death by drowning. He knew that political intrigues had caused him to be declared insane, and he was sure he had been murdered by a political group. Karl had tremendous insight about his choice to work in the mental health fields. He said, "I wasn't crazy. I was very sensitive, and I was set up to appear quite loony. The times I was locked up were just horrible. No wonder I'm absolutely terrified in the mental wards at times. But my problem lay in trusting the people who framed me. I was artistic and naive. I think I may have gone a bit unbalanced because of the betrayal. If there were only some way to set history straight about all that."

For both Karl and Lucinda, their present financial decisions lay in the German lifetime. Karl couldn't rest on his laurels in the present life. He had to work for the betterment of mankind's mental health. Lucinda was a gracious hostess when Karl visited her. She enjoyed shopping for food and cooking for Karl, and never let him know about her tight budget. Although she allowed him to take her to dinner many times, her joy was to feed and take care of Karl. Karl did not recognize Lucinda as a prostitute, but he knew he had been acquainted with her in the German lifetime. Lucinda preferred not to tell him about her past, even though it was a past life. Karl remains special in Lucinda's heart, even though they are no longer in touch with each other. Lucinda said, "Next life!"

Lucinda flashed on another life that might explain her concern about money and her reluctance to accept gifts or help from anyone. Her fierce independence was a blessing in this life, since she is determined to have success as an actress, but Lucinda confessed she worried about money all the time. Sometimes that was to the point of near paralysis. She suddenly saw herself as a young man on a ship. She said, "How glamorous! I'm a pirate! I think we board ships that are bound for the New World and take their cargo. There are only a few of us, so perhaps we go after small passenger ships and rob the people on board. I know where we hide the booty. It is somewhere off the coast of Spain or Portugal in a cave. I have a feeling that if I went to Spain and drove down the coast, I'd find the exact location. Some of those stolen goods must still be there. I believe this life comes as a result of the life of prostitution. I think I'm still very angry about the German lifetime in that I didn't have a normal family and some security. I suppose my wealthy clients are not so generous once I get older. Perhaps I die very poor, and now I'm determined to take what I can, when I can. Evidently, I don't think it is so bad to do what we're doing. It's like I say, 'Everyone has to do what they can to survive.'

"I am making up for that attitude now. I really don't want anything that doesn't belong to me, and I'm not ever envious of others' good fortune. I can honestly say I've never been jealous of success. I am determined to make it on my own in this life, and to do it the honest way."

Glenda had a more dramatic take on her present financial success. Glenda, an attractive advertising executive in her early fifties, made an appointment to see me. A man she loved deeply had just died. She had never been in a relationship with Charles, but there had been several painful near-misses when they might have been together. Glenda's relationship with Charles began when they were in college. She told me a bit of the background as she was reviewing the circumstances of her present life.

Glenda fell in love with Charles, after she had known him for several years. The tragedy was that Glenda was married, but her marriage had been in trouble from the very beginning. She met her husband, Joe, in college. After a few dates, she stopped seeing Joe and, soon afterward, became "pinned" to a college man, Al, in another fraternity. The act of being pinned was at least the same as "going steady," but not quite like being engaged. It all happened so fast that Glenda wasn't sure she knew her own mind. She was not sure she was really in love with Al, but she did recognize that she hurt Joe very much by ending their short relationship so abruptly. His obvious misery made her take a second look at her feelings for him. She gave the fraternity pin back to Al.

Joe was the kind of young man who kept his feelings to himself. He did not tell her he cared for her and behaved in such a nonchalant manner, she had no idea he really thought about her at all. However, Glenda decided the situation must have been a fated one, for she was pulled back into Joe's orbit again. Soon afterward, and without very much passion or prelude, Glenda discovered she was pregnant with Joe's baby. She had been a virgin and had been very sure she would remain so until her marriage. She was brought up very strictly by her parents and because of her academic record, she had a very strong future in front of her. Her first, and only, sexual encounter was nothing like she had read about or heard about. It was almost like it never happened, yet here she was ... pregnant. After an agonizing confession to her puritanical mother, she was shocked to realize that her family hinted at an option for her to have an abortion. They also hinted that she could go away to have the baby, who would then be put up for adoption. The most touching, but terrifying offer came from her sister, who had been married for almost ten years without being able to conceive. She almost automatically assumed that Glenda would be overjoyed for her to adopt the baby. Glenda was so horrified, she swallowed her pride and elected to marry someone she didn't love. She couldn't imagine giving up her baby, much less to her sister. She couldn't fathom seeing her own child all the time, pretending to be an aunt, when the baby would be brought up by someone else.

Her new financial future was very precarious, indeed. Joe had three more years of college ahead of him, and although he was a good student and very intelligent, he didn't seem to have a lot of ambition. Glenda decided that she would have to go back to work after her baby was born.

Soon after she had her adorable daughter, she started to talk to Charles at some of the college gatherings. She had been in his company many times, because he was one of her husband's close friends. She knew he was extremely intelligent and witty, but she had no way of knowing about his softer side. Charles revealed his romantic, sensitive nature when they started dancing together at fraternity parties. Charles was a wonderful dancer, as was Glenda, whereas Joe didn't like to dance at all. Joe didn't mind that Charles and Glenda enjoyed dancing together, but none of them realized that, little by little, Glenda and Charles were falling in love. Glenda was starved for affection, and Charles verbalized his feelings for her very beautifully. However, their sense of ethics was very strong, and they soon stopped dancing together. It was extremely painful for Glenda not to be with Charles, but they chose to be honorable in their behavior toward each other. Charles married another woman, Barbara, soon after meeting her, and although Glenda felt they were as mismatched as she and Joe, she had no further conversation with Charles.

Glenda had three major encounters with Charles throughout the next fifteen years. Once, after she was divorced from Joe, and Charles was divorced from Barbara, she called him and asked if they could meet. But the timing was wrong again. Charles was just about to announce his engagement to a beautiful woman named Allison. Glenda licked her wounds and went on with her life.

Joe died very suddenly before he was forty, and Glenda, although no longer married to him, attended his funeral. Their daughter was very attached to her father, even though she did not see him often, but their love kept Glenda in some kind of communication with Joe. She felt very sad about Joe's early death, especially for her daughter's sake. Charles was at the funeral and commented that Glenda looked well. His personal tragedy was that Allison, who looked like a goddess, was really a troubled young woman. She had spent a great deal of time in and out of mental hospitals. Charles had been responsible for raising his sons almost single-handedly. Glenda, quite naturally, felt deep regrets for him. So, several years later when Charles died as a result of a tragic accident, puzzlement over the sad timing in her relationship with Charles led her to make an appointment for a regression session with me.

Her first regression session uncovered a lifetime that was so dramatic, she knew there had to be more information lurking in her consciousness, so Glenda was able to view several past lives. She flashed on a Japanese lifetime where she knew she had been on-stage. She said, "I have a really hard time believing that I'm seeing something real, because it is the story of *Madame Butterfly*! I don't think I was Madame Butterfly, but because I'm an opera lover, I know the story quite well. I'm a small, but very beautiful Japanese girl in the theater. As far as I know the Kabuki theater had only male actors, but I see myself on-stage and know that I have a prominent reputation. It's different than now. It's as if I have been trained for this all my life, and it is not a matter of my making a decision about it. I'm locked in. I love it, of course. The terrible thing is that I fall in love with an English naval officer." Glenda paused and shook her head. "I promise I'm seeing this as if a film were running across my vision. I don't think I'm just copying the story of *Madame Butterfly*. Anyway, my family are just enraged and forbid me to see him. First of all, they look down on someone with white skin, and, secondly, I'm not supposed to have a personal life. They are absolutely rude toward him and forbid me to see him ever again when they realize we know each other. I believe he comes backstage to meet me after a performance.

"I think my mother and father are the same as in the present life. They are very, very strict, as is my family now. Of course they absolutely force me into his arms by making me hide our meetings. We have a sexual relationship, and we don't think about the consequences. We love each other so very much. I get pregnant, but I'm not sure he knows about it. He is shipped out before I have a chance to tell him. My family have rejected him so badly, he never contacts me again."

I asked Glenda if she recognized the English officer in the present life. She said, "Oh, my God, it is Joe, and it is the same as now, only backward. In this life, Joe's family treated me like dirt because I was pregnant and didn't lie about it. In spite of my own determination to keep the baby, Joe was very insistent that we be married. I might have thought he was the kind of man who wouldn't want the responsibility of a baby, but the opposite was true. He was very determined that we get married right away.

"Oh, I'm seeing something amazing. I have the baby, but must give it up for adoption. It is a little girl, too. My heart is breaking, but I'm bound to honor and obey my family. I have no choice or say in the matter. In this life, my mother was so nervous about my dating boys, she almost examined me with a microscope when I'd get home; it was as if she might see a fingerprint on my arm or body! I was such a good girl, but I think she forced me into Joe's arms, once again. She didn't like Joe at all in this life, either. She almost detested him, but once she knew we were going to get married, she changed dramatically. She was on his side after that, even when I knew I had to divorce him for my own sanity. She did a complete about-face."

Glenda continued, "Well, guess who adopted my baby? My family and I discreetly searched for a couple who wanted a child. We found two people who needed some money, but who we knew would really love and care for my little daughter. I was able to watch her grow up into a really beautiful young lady. The couple are my sister and brother-in-law in this life! No wonder my sister just expected I would want her to adopt my daughter now. I suffered a lot seeing that lovely girl and knowing that I could never tell her I was her mother. My story departs form the *Madame Butterfly* saga, because I did not commit suicide. I continued to earn my own money and was very successful. Maybe that's why I'm lucky enough to be able to only work in the theater and not have to augment my income with work I'm really not interested in."

Glenda needed some time to digest this incredibly detailed past-life memory. She said she felt sadness for Joe in that lifetime and could understand so much about his behavior in the present time. Joe was an alcoholic in the present time. That was one of the reasons Glenda felt she couldn't stay married to him. She added, "I think my English officer drank quite a lot to drown his sorrows in the Japanese lifetime." After a moment she said, "I can't believe it, but I have a picture of Joe as a child, dressed in a little white suit. It is almost a replica of the uniform he wore as an officer.

"The other startling thing is that in that lifetime I earned my own money. In the present time, I am more successful than Joe, and I supported myself and my daughter totally. Joe never gave me money for child support, and I didn't ask for any. I almost didn't want him to contribute to our welfare. I have been 'liberated' about money long before it was popular. I have always thought that unless there was a great deal of money in a family, a woman was morally bound to contribute what she could to the support of the family. I was a bit critical of women who only spent time in beauty parlors, or indulging themselves, even if they were married. I have always admired women who built a career of their own."

Glenda had satisfied her need to understand her relationship to Joe, but she had not placed Charles in her past lives. It was Charles' death that motivated Glenda to seek a regression session in the first place.

I directed Glenda to go to another life where she might have known Charles. The first thing she said was, "Oh, what a beautiful house. I've seen pictures of just such a house in magazines. It is very European and very grand. The windows are beautiful . . . floor to ceiling . . . with gorgeous draperies inside, and on the outside there are tasteful cement carvings everywhere around the doors and windows. It is like a small castle. It seems to have small turrets and corners, and the statuary and landscaping is just fabulous. Evidently this is a lifetime of affluence. I have many servants to take care of everything, and I am married to a man I just adore. It is Charles. Oh, I love him so much. We don't have any children, but I seem to be quite young, perhaps in my mid-twenties. There is a painful situation with my husband . . . a tragedy. I believe he is killed shortly after the scene in my mind.

"I see him on horseback, getting ready to go off somewhere to join a group of men. It's not quite an army, but more like volunteers who are going to quell some sort of uprising. I believe there is a campaign or small skirmish that must be cleared up. I don't think this is too long ago . . . perhaps in the late 1800s. I'm not even sure he has to participate in this event, but he has a strong sense of duty. I think he is a bit of a daredevil as well. That's what scares me so. I'm afraid he'll be foolishly reckless. I see myself reaching up for a last hug and kiss, and we just cling to each other. I'm very upset over his leaving me. We are really devoted to each other.

"Now I see myself in my older years. I think I live a long time after he dies. I must be about the age I am now, but I am very sad and subdued. I almost appear to be older, yet my face is still young. I think I never leave my house. I do needlepoint and read, but have absolutely no social life. I mourn him all the rest of my life. My servants take care of me and my needs, but I don't really get close to any of them. Oh, there is so much I could do in that life. I have money and help. I have plenty of free time and no family to care for. Why don't I do some kind of charitable work? Why don't I start an orphanage, or help the poor and needy? Do you think my indulgence in my own sorrow has been the reason I couldn't be with Charles in this life? I might easily have done little else with my life other than take care of him if we had been together in the present. But that wouldn't have been so bad, I don't think. No wonder I'm so judgmental about women who do nothing with their lives. What a waste."

In a short time, Glenda added, "There is another factor. I think Charles never stopped beating himself up, in his soul consciousness or on a spiritual plane. I think he saw how sad he made me then by leaving me, and I think, somehow, we both stopped ourselves from being together. We might have been very self-centered and could have neglected any sense of community duty, or contribution we might make to others if we'd been sublimely happy again."

CHAPTER 8

Past-life abuse;
sexual problems now.

Almost all physical weaknesses and conditions can be traced to past-life situations. Sexual dysfunction is only one of many physical disabilities that have their roots in the past. For example, if an individual has a propensity toward heart problems, he or she may see a past-life death by being stabbed in the heart.

A young lady born with multiple sclerosis saw herself as a man in a recent time. She was a very well-known Jewish scientist and professor in her last lifetime, living in Germany during World War II. She was on the verge of discovering a cure for a common but fatal disease when she was taken to a concentration camp. She was gassed along with other Jewish victims.

Part of the horror of the manner of her death was the suddenness with which the penalty was levied. She was told that she was going to work with the Germans in a scientific research program, and she, reluctantly but with relief, went with the Germans to the camp. She was tricked at the last minute and led into the showers. The terror and shock she felt over the betrayal left her to die with tremendous fear that lodged in her nervous system. Although she may not be able to find a cure for multiple sclerosis, this beautiful and intelligent young lady can at least comprehend why she, but not other members of her family, should be born with the disease. Lara was born with very high intelligence and a scientific mind. Perhaps Lara will make inroads in research that will help eventually help other victims of her disease.

Sexual dysfunction in the present time may be directly related to past-life violence of some sort. The dysfunction can be traced to past lives spent in warlike or violent situations, as an example. Usually a person went beyond what was expected of him or her in war in a past life, enjoying the brutality he or she used against another person. This is when the karmic punishment of present-life sexual dysfunction is most apparent. If we look back over history, and recognize the level of violence that prevailed during most of those important eras, it is no wonder that sexual dysfunction can be such a major problematic area in troubled relationships.

SEXUAL VIOLENCE IN CHILDHOOD

Helen's penalty for past-life violence seems overly tragic in her present existence. On the day of her scheduled appointment, I had opened the door to the terrace for a bit of fresh air on a balmy spring day in New York. I had planned to shut the door as soon as Helen arrived, in case it might turn chilly during our session. Helen greeted me and immediately asked me to close the door. She apologized, saying she was always very cold. I shut the door and found a knitted afghan to put around her shoulders. Helen was extremely thin. She had a haunted look about her eyes and made no attempt to cover her anxiety with any small talk. She was clearly intent on the work that we were to do together.

In response to my first question, Helen told me about an incident that had occurred when she was around the age of eleven. She was visiting her beloved grandmother, her father's mother, and her adored Uncle Josh, a bachelor who was still living at home. Uncle Josh spent a lot of time with Helen and gave her special attention that was not lavished on her brothers and sisters. These periodic visits to her extended family were very important to Helen.

Helen saw herself standing by the apartment window at twilight, looking out on the cold, snowy New York scene below her, when Uncle Josh came over to stand behind her. When he put his arms around her, Helen suddenly began screaming in terror. Uncle Josh backed away from her immediately and led her away from the window. As he sat her down on the living room couch he kneeled beside her and gently caressed her hand. He was devastated and said, "Darling, what is the matter? You know I would not hurt you. Why were you screaming?"

In the panic of the moment, Helen's carefully guarded secret tumbled out. Without being able to stop herself, she told her uncle of the terror of being raped by her father, Josh's brother. Uncle Josh made an effort to be calm as he heard the news and tried to extend that calm to Helen. Helen realized that she had just done the very thing she had sworn she would never do. She immediately regretted her outburst, but she had simply been unable to stop herself from telling. Helen's father had warned her, repeatedly, that if she ever revealed anything about these episodes, something terrible would happen. Her father said that he would denounce her before their church and expose the devil that was in her body. Everyone would know her for a liar and a witch.

Helen begged her uncle to protect her secret and, especially, to keep it from her grandmother. After a long while, Uncle Josh was able to reassure Helen, and he gave her some hot chocolate to drink. He said he wanted to take a short walk, but that he would be back soon. He promised, again, not to divulge anything to anyone.

Sometime later, Helen heard Uncle Josh calling to her. She went to the door, but he was not there. It was now growing quite dark, and Helen went in to be with her grandmother in the kitchen. Uncle Josh had been gone a very long time by now, and Helen and her grandmother wondered where he might be.

When the telephone rang, it was up to Helen to pick up the receiver, as her grandmother didn't understand English. Helen hoped it was Uncle Josh, but instead it was a stranger who informed her that her uncle had been taken to the hospital. The stranger was finally forced to tell Helen that Uncle Josh was dead. He had either slipped or had committed suicide by jumping from the roof of the building.

In addition to the devastating shock and panic she felt, Helen had to break the news to her grandmother. But the horrifying thought that ran through her head was that Daddy was right. Uncle Josh's death was proof that her father's prophecy had come true. She had told someone about the bad things in her life, and now something much worse had happened. Helen was left with the sure knowledge that she had killed her beloved Uncle Josh, and she took full responsibility in her own mind. She would have to live with the guilt for the rest of her life. She could bear that pain, but nothing could ever persuade her to tell of it again.

After her uncle's death, Helen's hair began falling out. Finally, a school counselor began to worry about her and called a psychologist to interview her. During the session, Helen was given some puzzles to do as the psychologist asked her some questions. Concentrating on the task before her, she automatically answered everything quite truthfully. It seemed that she told the psychologist about the sexual abuse without being aware of what she was saying. When she realized what she had done, she was absolutely frozen with fear and felt anger at being tricked by the man and those puzzles.

Helen's mother was called to come to the school, and Helen was terrified of what might happen when her mother arrived. It was decided that Helen must take a compulsory trip to the hospital. At the emergency room, the physical examination revealed severe internal damage. In fact, the damage was so extensive, it was imperative to remove Helen's appendix along with a lot of scar tissue. Since the situation had now come under the scrutiny of the school authorities, the courts would not allow Helen to come home before her father was barred from entering the house. Something terrible had happened again.

Helen's mother blamed Helen for ruining not only her marriage, but her whole future. The family life had obviously been completely disrupted, and it was Helen's fault. Eventually their house had to be sold. In spite of the evidence, Helen's mother staunchly defended her husband. Helen was denounced, not to the church, but to the family, for Helen's mother told the other children that Helen was lying.

The repercussions extended to Helen's grandmother. She was hospitalized for a very long time and lost her eyesight. Helen called the condition "traumatic blindness," resulting from shock or trauma. During one of Helen's visits to the hospital, her grandmother begged Helen to tell her the truth. Helen said she had been lying, for she was quite certain that if she told her grandmother the truth, her beloved grandmother would die.

Finally, when Helen was about fifteen years old, one of her brothers confirmed her story. He told her that he knew what had happened. He had discovered their father raping Helen on the kitchen floor with a handkerchief stuffed in her mouth. The layout of the house included a spiral staircase leading from the kitchen to a basement playroom. At times Helen's father would send the other children down the stairs to play, but he would keep Helen with him.

One day the boy crept up the stairs and saw what was happening. He was afraid to defend Helen when she was accused of lying. Before his admission, Helen lived in a hell of isolation, completely alone in her knowledge of what had occurred. Her mother did such a convincing job of branding her a liar, she was ostracized by the family. No one believed her, and she had no one to defend her. After her brother's admission to Helen, he stopped speaking to his mother. As soon as Helen herself refused to see her mother, her hair stopped falling out.

There were many suicide attempts. When Helen was about fifteen, she almost succeeded. In fact, she was pronounced dead by her doctors. Her recovery was deemed miraculous, as she had been brain-dead so long it was fully expected that she would be in a vegetative state. During her near-death experience, Helen had a visit with Uncle Josh. In that visitation, Uncle Josh convinced her to return to life to fulfill her mission. Helen had an illegitimate child at an early age, but after many years in therapy she met and married a kind, loving man. Her marriage proved to be a happy experience.

In the regression session, when Helen went back to another lifetime, she saw herself as a woman wearing a uniform. She identified that garment as a Nazi uniform, and saw herself as part of a twosome. Her vision produced the sight of running down a street with a gun in her hand along with her boyfriend, also in uniform. They both seemed to delight in their role as snipers. Helen described the street scene and the buildings quite vividly, as well as the alleyways where they would hide. The area appeared to be a ghetto. Helen felt tremendous gusto when she was killing men, women, and children. Coupled with that thrill came violent and wild sexual urges. She and her partner alternately indulged in killing and then unrestrained, orgiastic sex. Together they killed hundreds of people.

Eventually, I asked Helen if she knew that man in her present life. Her affirmative response led me to ask if she could identify him. It came as no surprise to me that she named her father as her former lover. The violence and the attraction had repeated itself in this life. Group karma came into play as she tried to identify some of the people they had killed. She quickly saw her mother as one of her former victims. She knew she had to contact her mother again, and although she might not be able to tell her mother about her regression session, her changed attitude could not help but bring a truce between them, if not a full healing.

In her mind's eye, if Helen could ask her mother's forgiveness for Nazi Germany and could forgive herself, her mother might forgive Helen for what she saw as Helen's treachery and, more importantly, acknowledge her betrayal of Helen in this life. All of this can be accomplished without saying anything about past lives to the other person. Thoughts are very potent if accompanied by sincere emotion and feeling. Helen went back to another past life. This time she saw a life as a devoted healer in an Egyptian temple. Her particular task was working with people who had animallike appendages.

Plastic surgery was quite common in ancient Egypt. That practice had come from Atlantis along with some survivors of the great flood. The major difference between ancient and modern-day plastic surgery was the motivation. Much of present-day plastic surgery is an attempt toward the beautification and recapture of youth. Egyptian plastic surgery was an attempt to correct the corrupt Atlantean practice of breeding humans with animals to create an obvious slave class. Throughout the ages from Atlantis to ancient Egypt, the genetic experimentation had left some people with an extra appendage, such as a tail. Helen's job was to help in the removal of those extraneous parts of the body.

Helen now has strong examples of the choice between the high road and the low. It is obvious that the guilt on a soul level caused a tremendous amount of pain in Helen's present life. More self-punishment cannot restore the balance of right and wrong on a soul-consciousness level, but self-forgiveness can. My suggestion to Helen was that ultimate self-forgiveness had to relate not only to the acts committed in Germany, but to the awareness of the slide from the highest level of consciousness to the lowest. The climb back up to the high side of spiritual awareness and into the light is often a difficult and treacherous journey. How can one forgive oneself for such short-sighted stupidity? Better to never have climbed the heights than to make a wrong turn to a fall. The painful struggle throughout an eternity of lives to stand again in the light and balance the scales may be a hard price to pay. If one possesses an evolved state of consciousness, it demands an even greater sense of responsibility.

I asked Helen if she thought she had suffered enough in this life. There was no need for her to answer that question. She knows she has been more than sufficiently chastised on a soul-consciousness level. She can allow herself to begin her true work in this life. Helen also has a vision of the mission she is to fulfill, as foretold by Uncle Josh. She is already beginning her training as a therapist. Since the ultimate purpose of a regression session is to effect healing, such healing can only occur when an individual can forgive himself on a conscious level for what was formerly buried in the unconscious mind. In Helen's situation, the awareness of the brutal acts she committed in Nazi Germany was somewhat balanced by her awareness of the positive, healing efforts in Egypt. This may sound amazingly pat and easy. Only the individual going through the day-by-day healing process can know the depth of its reality.

TRANSEXUALITY

Donna is an attractive, well-groomed young lady with an optimistic, outgoing personality. Although she has a sense of humor and a philosophical attitude, Donna has a serious side, too. She's clearly a hardworking, diligent person with a sense of responsibility about life. Donna acknowledged that she had always had a need to find her life's work. She cannot ignore a desire to fulfill an inborn sense of destiny.

When Donna arrived, I was unaware that she had undergone a sex-change operation. I was somewhat surprised, as her appearance was totally feminine. It had been difficult for Donna to make the decision to have the operation, but she felt the change from male to female would correct a mistake nature made in putting her in a male body. As Donna began to review difficult or traumatic moments in the present life, she discussed the events that led up to her decision to become a woman. She felt she would be much happier if she could live in a feminine body, because it seemed to be more fitting for the realization of her destiny, whatever that might be.

Donna was an easy person to work with, but her tears revealed the depths of her suffering in the present life. When she began to review past lives, she quickly saw herself as a baby boy of four or five months. She knew she had been murdered just a year before she was reborn into this lifetime. It seemed that she had been born to a young, heavyset, unmarried girl who lived alone in the Boston area. Donna knew the girl was a drug addict. When Donna described her surroundings as the second floor of an unused carriage house near Beacon Hill, she said, "The space is so dirty that when I crawl around, filthy particles stick to my neck and it hurts. But I don't dare complain." The young girl, Donna's mother, was clearly unequipped to take care of herself, much less her baby boy. She was in a perilous situation and felt very burdened having a child to look after. Donna realized that as the baby boy, he couldn't even cry. The woman was so out of control, it would be dangerous to protest. Donna knew she had lived in constant fear of being injured. She described the situation by saying, "I'm afraid of her. She's stronger than I am, and I have to be very careful."

The girl was involved with a man who did not want the responsibility for a baby, especially one who was not his own child. The man decided to leave the area, and the girl had to make a choice. It was either him or her child. Since she had no love for the baby anyway, the decision was clear. Donna realized that the thing he (the baby) dreaded most was about to happen. He was going to be badly hurt. It was early in the evening, and the baby was lying in his crib. As soon as the girl came into the room, Donna knew what was to take place. She said, "I'm not sorry she kills me. Before she puts the pillow over my face, I know she's going to do something to me. When she enters the room, I know the time has come. When she puts the pillow over my face, I leave my body very quickly. It's like going up in an elevator. It's funny that all this time I was afraid of being hurt, but when the time comes, I want to leave just as much as she wants me to go."

I asked Donna if the young mother has any remorse. She replied, "No, none at all." When I asked Donna why she had to be born to that woman in the first place, she went to another lifetime where she was a young boy approximately four years old. She saw the child in a courtyard playing with his sisters. Then Donna saw him standing at a wall watching a lot of horses on a road. They were making quite a bit of noise, but the young boy was not afraid. The horses belonged to his father, who was an English nobleman and part of the landed gentry at the time of the War of the Roses. There was a wonderful feeling of security as the boy played with his pretty blond sisters and his mother, an important lady in her own right. His home was beautiful, and life seemed ideal.

But matters changed drastically when the father went off to war. He was a daring man and was soon killed in battle. Without the father at home to take care of matters, the estate began to deteriorate. It soon fell into a state of dilapidation. Donna realized that all the women in the family looked to him to be strong for them, and to take on the role of the man of the house. As a four-year-old child, he was totally unprepared for that job. Donna described the situation and said, "I'm just too young. I don't feel man enough to shoulder that load. My mother is not a strong woman, and shortly after my father's death, she begins to decline. There is no one there to teach me or show me what to do, I take on all the guilt for my mother's apathy and for the ruin of the estate. I feel like a total failure. I simply, passively, let it all go. I never marry in that life, and I finally die in my room around the age of forty. I think my death comes as a total lack of interest in anything, even in living. It is like a suicide of loneliness and neglect."

Donna began to make some connections between that lifetime and the present one. She said, "Oh, my father in that lifetime is my father now." There was a long pause before she continued. "He didn't provide for me then, and I didn't want him as my father figure in this life. I don't learn how to become a man in that life, as I didn't know my father well enough before he died. I felt more like the women then. When my father didn't come back to our home in England, I wanted the women to protect me, instead of expecting me to be strong for them.

"In this lifetime, I was born into a family where the women are strong. At least I could learn to be a person through their influence. My father doesn't live up to his fatherly duties in this life, either." I asked Donna to examine her feelings about her father then and now. She replied, "I blamed him and hated him in England, and I've wanted to kill him in this life." I asked her how she could resolve her feelings toward her father. She replied, "When one is inadequate like my father, it is necessary for me to develop the compassion I need to forgive him for his lack of courage in this life and for his lack of strategy and cunning in the English life. He charged into battle then and lost his life, which left us alone. I can understand why he has no courage now."

Then Donna said, "Oh! My little sister in the English life was very angry with me because I let her down. She was the mother in Boston who murdered me! It's funny that even though the young woman was victimizing me, and even when she killed me, I felt like it was a punishment." I asked Donna if she felt that her sex-change operation was, even on the most subtle level, a way of getting even with her father. She replied, very quietly, "Yes."

Since Donna recognized that she was not really getting the most out of her feminine self in this lifetime, I asked her if there had ever been a strong life as a female. She said, "I see myself standing on a hill in the early evening. I seem to be wearing a Grecian dress with a robe, I'm holding a small casket, or box. It appears to be on Mykonos, and I'm a priestess. I have guardianship of the sacred object. It holds information that is very powerful, and my role is to protect this information. But I am also able to indoctrinate certain people if I think they are ready to have this information. I must be about thirty years old. Someone is riding by on a horse and jumps me from behind. Oh, no! I'm murdered again when he punctures my heart with a sharp object. After I die, however, he is stricken with grief and remorse." Donna paused, "It's the man I'm involved with now. We have a good relationship in this life, and he feels a strong responsibility for me. I can see my spirit hovering over him in that life. I feel great sympathy for him. I'm afraid he's going to open the box and then he will have to deal with what he learns, karmically. I see him reading and reading. I know he'll have to guard this knowledge, so I pledge myself to be with him so that we'll be tied together for many lives. My guilt is that I wasn't careful enough in my guardianship of that sacred object. I don't feel as if I gave him much of a fight or struggle then. That must have started an apathetic tendency in my personality and in future lives."

I gave Donna some input on what I saw. It appeared to me that the female part of her is in danger of being killed, and that it is difficult to allow that side to emerge fully in the present time. I suggested that she may need to form and develop the feminine side of herself a little longer. I asked her to see how she punished that woman for the neglect of her duties and asked if she had suffered enough. Donna replied, "I think so. The problem was that she was prideful. She was trying for something more than what she already had, and she had quite a lot. She tried to rush things and was being delinquent and a bit arrogant by standing on the hilltop too long."

I suggested that she look at the lifetimes in review. The first one was when she was neglected as a young boy. As a grown man, in turn, he neglected his responsibilities. The second life was when he was killed as a baby. But then, in a lifetime as a female in Greece, she was again killed. Donna replied, "The female part says, 'I'm the strong one here, and the wise one. I'm the spiritual one, but I may be killed if I'm not careful.' " I asked why she was not born female in this life. She replied, "I needed to climb back to reach that higher realm. I could only do it by being close to the ground and being in a male body. It's like having to crawl from rock to rock without being able to leap from one to the other. I'm a little scared now, because I think the female part of me is ready to emerge completely."

VICTIMS OF INCEST

Samuel is a young man who has been in therapy for many years. One of the reasons for the extensive therapy was the extreme loneliness he felt throughout his whole life. He came to me for a regression session in order to gain further insight into his life situation. In reviewing childhood in this life, Samuel revealed that he had been sexually abused by his father when he was a baby. It is horrifying to realize that incest is more common than one might expect. Some parents seem to think they own their children and can do whatever they like with them. Samuel is just one such victim of a father's lust.

Samuel's brother Carl recommended that he come to me for a regression session. It had been several years since Carl's session, but I remembered Carl with fondness. The review of his past lives were quite profound and brought a deep release for him. He thought his brother could be helped in the same way.

However, as Samuel reviewed the loneliness of his life, in spite of a moderately large-sized family—a mother, father, and three boys—it was apparent that a deep-seated sadness could not be abated by any amount of companionship. As a young boy, Samuel was not allowed to play with other children, or to explore his neighborhood. He wasn't permitted to do the usual things a boy of his age might do. He was not allowed to run errands for his mother, play ball in the park, or go away to Boy Scout camp, for example. Samuel's boredom caused him to watch television when other children were out playing. His restlessness was hardly satisfied by that activity. He saw himself, at age twelve, sniffing glue to get high; something he couldn't experience naturally through challenging adventures. Then Samuel saw himself at age seven in the basement of the apartment building where he lived. His father was the superintendent of the building, and called Samuel to come down and join him. In response to my question about what was happening next, Samuel said, "I can't say it. I just can't say it." It took some gentle persuasion, and reassurance, to convince Samuel that I already knew what he was seeing so he could safely verbalize what was going on. Finally he said, "It's very bad, and I'm to blame.

"My father is telling me that he wants to teach me about women. He's asking me to examine his penis and play with it." I asked Samuel if his father also touched him, and he said, "Yes." I didn't press Samuel for details, but I asked him to tell me why he felt he was so bad. He said he was ashamed of the pleasure he felt and knew he had great guilt at the same time. The pleasure overweighed the guilt, and Samuel didn't stop his father.

When Samuel went to a past life, he saw himself in a female body in an Arabian culture. She was married to a man she loved very much and was surrounded by opulence. However, the man was very jealous of his beautiful wife and kept her locked in a room. Her servants could bring her food and sweetmeats, or anything her heart desired, but she had no freedom. One night when her husband came to her room for lovemaking, the woman stabbed him with a knife she had concealed under her pillow. Samuel had no need to understand his life in another way when he identified that husband as his father in the present time. His response was one I had heard many times before. "This makes so much sense and explains my whole life."

CROSS-DRESSING

Peter is a charming, sensitive, and artistic young man with a happy home life. He is married, for the second time, to a vibrant, successful actress. His children by his first wife accept their stepmother and love them both. When Peter called me for a regression session, it appeared as though he had no serious problems to resolve. However, Peter tends to take the weight of the world on his shoulders. He feels a sense of destiny about his life. Peter was born with what I call an "Atlas complex."

Peter evidently developed a strong sense of responsibility from an early age, and it could become quite burdensome at times. He also periodically suffered from intense depression. His sense of duty was reinforced by mandates from both parents as he was growing up. Peter's mother and father did not have a happy marriage. Somehow, Peter felt responsible for their unhappiness. Since I always look at an astrological chart before I do a regression session, I notice that Peter also has what I call "homicidal rage." A person with this aspect in his chart always appears to be extremely easygoing, looking on the surface as if butter would melt in his or her mouth.

However, the problem with having such a level of anger comes from an inability to release it. The person has never been able to struggle in some area of life in order to release the frustrations that continue to build. It is frightening for the individual to express his or her anger, so negative energies internalize, sometimes causing health problems. It is like sitting on an atomic bomb that might explode any moment. When we started the session, Peter was unaware, consciously, of the level of anger that he feels toward his mother. He discovered all about that later on and confirmed the internalization of his frustrations with her.

Peter described himself as a small child of three, sitting at the top of the staircase in the lobby of his apartment building. He was looking down on three people deep in a conversation. His mother and father were having an intense discussion with a man whom Peter knows as Alan. Then his mother and the man went off together. His father took him back into their apartment and asked a telling question. "Who do you love most? Me or Alan?" Naturally Peter replied, "You."

Then Peter saw himself in a crib in his own room at around age two. There was a party in his parents' apartment to celebrate the ending of the war, but Peter was left in the room, alone, in his crib. Evidently a guest had been in to visit Peter and had left some matches within Peter's reach. Peter did what one might anticipate a two-year-old to do. With some of the matches, he started a fire. His mother reacted as one might anticipate and scolded him soundly, again leaving him alone in his room at the end of her tirade. Although Peter's sister came to play with him, he felt quite rebuffed by his mother's reaction. At age two, Peter saw himself shutting down all systems in his body . . . heart, mind, and feelings.

With some examination of the incident, Peter realized that he was bored, and the matches represented some excitement. It was only in our session that Peter realized it was a way to get even with his mother for excluding him from the festivities. He knew he wasn't just trying to get her attention. He could release some anger and frustrations by causing her to be upset. Peter got a good reaction from his mother. Sometimes, unconsciously, any reaction is better than none at all. Of course the end result was that all his actions only backfired. Peter was still left in his room. Now he also felt very sad and rejected. In Peter's case it resulted in a lifetime of cutting off from feelings.

Peter then saw himself as a nine-month-old baby. Peter's mother and father were having a raging argument in the room that Peter shared with his mother and sister. (Peter's mother had already moved out of the father's room by the time Peter was nine months old.) Peter's mother was changing his diaper, and during the course of the argument, she inadvertently was quite rough with Peter, sticking him with her fingernails and with a pin. Peter protested her lack of attention by squirming and crying, and only caused himself more pain in the long run. His mother punished him severely for protesting. Peter saw that he was not allowed to struggle. His anger, once again, was internalized. I asked Peter to look inside his body to see where the anger was lodged. He hesitated for some time and then replied, "The genitals." Incidents in early life, such as Peter recalled, can predescribe later sexual behavior. Peter, as a little baby, was so angry that he began to relate sexuality with anger, especially because his mother was rough about changing his diapers. In an extreme case, this may cause later tendencies to do something violent if the rage continues to build.

Suddenly Peter told me about a problem he has in his present life. He said, "I like to cross-dress and wear women's clothing occasionally. My wife knows about this, but it is something I don't understand.

I'm not gay. I have been to many psychiatrists to try to figure out why this desire persists!" I asked Peter to go to a time that might explain this. He flashed on a scene when he was about two years old. His mother was putting him to bed and dressed him in her silk slip. This may have happened many times, but Peter realized that this was almost the only time when Mother give him positive attention. His mother and sisters would hug him and tell him how cute he looked. Peter also loved the feel of the silk next to his skin. He said, "No wonder. It's almost the only time my mother is warm and nice to me."

When we went to a past life in an attempt to understand why all of this should have occurred in the first place, Peter saw himself as a young man in the Midwest. He was tall, good-looking, and very much a ladies' man. He seemed to be successful, judging by his appearance and the kind of clothes he wore. Peter saw himself frequenting a particular brothel in a small frontier town. The ladies of the night loved to have him visit them, and they showered him with attention. One day Peter met a young woman who was new in town. She had recently moved to the area from an East Coast city. She was extremely unhappy, and did not respond to Peter's advances. As Peter watched a scene unfold before his eyes, he knew that he had made improper advances toward the young lady, because of her very determined resistance to his overtures. He was standing outside a cabin where a celebration or party was going on, and the young lady stepped outside to get a breath of fresh air. Peter tried to kiss her, and as she struggled, a man came out of the house. He told Peter to stop. Peter's anger got the best of him, and he drew a gun, just to warn the man to mind his own business. The other man was also armed and, without any further warning, fired a shot. The young lady was suddenly in front of Peter and was killed instantly. In the scuffle, Peter had tried to push her out of the way, but she stepped in front of him instead. Peter knew it was an accident, but he blamed himself for losing control. When he took a look at the young woman, he knew it was his mother in the present life. It seemed she was still trying to get even with Peter for ending her life. The man holding the gun was, of course, Peter's father in the present life. Peter knew his first step was to beg his mother for forgiveness. Instead of needing an apology from his mother for her resistance to him in the present time, it was the other way around. He saw very clearly that he was the one who needed to show love and kindness to her.

CHAPTER 9

Past-life betrayal;
present-life antagonism.

Laura is an incredibly exciting woman who exudes a quality of electrical energy. She has achieved prominence in her chosen career as a fashion publisher. But, though she is a prime force in the fashion world, Laura's reputation is confined to the fashion industry rather than extending to areas in which she might be an influence on an even larger scale. In her regression session, she discovered a reason for this as well as a karmic relationship that needs to be resolved in her present life. In her chart, Saturn is placed in the seventh house of marriage and rules the fifth house of children. Laura's marriage ended painfully. She was left with the total support of three children, who rarely saw their father after the divorce. Uranus is the most elevated planet in her chart, positioned in the ninth house at the most potent spot in the zodiac; that is, just before the midheaven or Zenith of the wheel. Uranus rules her sixth house of work, indicating a great deal of fame arising from work in exciting areas involving publicity, promotional efforts, publishing, and international affairs. But as long as Laura allows the painful karmic memories of a past life to stop her, she will pick karmic relationships that give her an excuse to stop short of ultimate achievement. For instance, although Laura's children gave her a very strong motivation to succeed, she never traveled very far away from them because of her devotion to them. However, this may have caused her to miss opportunities to expand.

Before revealing an important event from a past life, Laura talked about an experience in this life. "I'm three years old. My mother has been gone for a long time. I'm told to sit still and wait for her to return. When she returns, I expect her to bring some warmth with her, but the room is still bare. This is a hotel room. (We came to the United States from England when I was only eighteen months old.) I see my mother but I can't touch her, because she's so removed. She's going through a lot of pain. She's trying to be strong, because my father has disappeared again. Actually he disappeared before I was born, so he hasn't been around very much. I'm feeling very sad about my father. No one has explained to me where he is. I don't understand why he's left me. He's very nurturing to me, and I need him. It upsets me so much when he leaves." Evidently Laura's mother had left her alone while she was looking for work. Part of Laura's pain came from the fact that her mother was so sad and frightened.

She went to an earlier moment that was very frightening to her. "I see myself on the boat coming to America from England. The voyage is rough, and

I'm very seasick. It's unclear why I'm on this boat in the first place. It's turbulent, and I don't like it. The room is down below, and it's dark. I sleep a lot and am very anxious. My mother is comforting and protective on this trip, so it feels like the two of us against the world. I'm out on deck in a stroller only a few times. I look at the people, and I like that, but I feel strange. I don't really want to get involved with them. I'm a bit indifferent, and I'm feeling a little bit superior. There is also an inner feeling of not fitting in. Outwardly I want to be part of the group, but something else is going on inside.

"My mother is very frightened. She's hanging on to me. It's funny, but I feel stronger and bigger than she is. I'm her security. She's frightened of what she's doing. I feel sorry for her, and I'd like to help her if I could. It's very chaotic when we arrive. There's no sense of purpose, and we don't know anyone. She's reckless but also frightened, so I'm frightened, too. I'm less patient, so I express my fears by crying. I'm feeling very unhappy. She's impatient, so she starts to put up a wall between us. When we arrive in the United States, she has no job and she doesn't have any money at all. She's running around everywhere, futilely. She's frantic. We go lots of places and look at things, but the tension is very hard to take."

After Laura's review of her birth, she looked at a past life that would give her an explanation for the circumstances of her present life. She said, "The people are poor. They have on brown tunics and rope belts, with cutoff pants and closed shoes. I'm sitting in a chair, and am wearing satin. I have a big round ring with a clear or gray stone. I'm a bit embarrassed by the ring. It seems gaudy and not a bit attractive, but it's supposed to be worn. My trousers seem to be a light gray or green. They are breeches, and I have on stockings. My jacket has buttons down the front. Obviously I am a man. I seem thin, but as I look down at my hands and ring, they seem gross to me. My body doesn't seem to fit my hand. There's some conflict with my wanting to be there. I'd like to be one of the women at the court because they are well taken care of. I don't like all the responsibility I have. It's very heavy, and there's a lot to do. It's never-ending. The women sit around in pretty dresses, and it's easy.

"I'm married, but my wife is just a fixture. There are some flirtations . . . but I don't think I want to look at that. Oh! I just had the wildest thought. I see the face of my daughter in this life framed by a hat. We have been lovers. But it is a real love! There is anger and frustration, sadness and jealousy. I love her to pieces. She's one of the women at the court. At this particular moment, it seems a flirtation. She's very young . . . about sixteen. I'm thirty. When I look into her eyes, it seems as though I can see through to her soul. Ah . . . we're not lovers yet. I'm so bored with the people sitting at my feet, and then I look across at this young girl and I have an immediate attraction. I want to plot and plan to find out about her, and how to woo her.

"I see her with me on a giant-sized bed with a very ornate canopy. She's in a beautiful white nightdress. I've summoned her, and she's intrigued, but she is not here of her own free will. I asked for her, and I got her. She has no choice, but she's intrigued. It is supposed to be just a young girl for an amusement, but when I look in her eyes, I fall in love. So I change from just wanting to make love to her to wanting to court her. I want to treat her kindly and with understanding. I don't make love to her that evening. I talk to her and touch her hair and comfort her. She's only a child, and she's afraid. I take care of her. After she has been with me for a while, I call someone to take her away safely. The love develops slowly because she's the only one I could love. She finally falls in love with me, but more slowly than I. I see her many times before she's responsive. I care too much for her to force her."

I asked Laura to describe herself a bit more. She said, "I'm not handsome at all, but I'm strong and charismatic and very persuasive." I asked her what happened to her love affair with this young girl. She responded, "We do become lovers. For a while it is idyllic. Then the nastiness comes in. People are jealous. I get overly involved in the relationship, and I don't see that people are taking advantage of me. In fact, there are a lot of things I don't see. Suddenly the thing that was so beautiful becomes a problem. My wife is very angry. She's not overly emotional about it, but she is angry and judgmental. It's an inconvenience to her. She doesn't understand that I love this person."

I asked Laura to describe her wife in that life. She said, "She's Spanish, and very dark." I asked her if she recognized her in the present life. She replied, "Oh, it's my mother!" I then suggested that she look around the court to see if she recognized anyone else. She replied, "My boyfriend in the present is one of the young pages in the court. We laugh and giggle and have fun. We communicate very well. He's a nice friend. He is warning me to be more careful, but I don't listen. He's too young to be advising me. But he tells me that I have an enemy."

I asked Laura to describe the degree of danger this enemy represented. She answered, "It's dangerous to go to sleep at night. The man is waiting for the right moment to do something. He's plotting and planning something. He pretends to be a friend. He's older and experienced in the ways of the court. He knows protocol, and he starts manipulating the people around me." Laura paused for a moment and then continued sadly, "He kills my young lover and therefore he has killed me, too. I die because I don't want to live anymore. The dynasty passes to his line."

Suddenly Laura gasped, "This is too easy. My enemy is my husband in this life. He hurt my daughter all over again. She used to be afraid of him, but she's able to handle him a bit better now that she is older. I came back to get revenge on him. If I destroy him in this life, however, it will just keep on going. How can I forgive him for what he did to us then? I guess in this life, he helped me make some small steps upward, whereas in that life, he helped me to death. I must learn how to handle him and must refuse to get into games with him; I need to develop a positive kind of apathy. By that I mean I must be attentive but not let him get to me. Most of all, I must be aware of what he is capable of doing in this life."

Laura and I discussed the intricate web of relationships that exist from one lifetime to another. In this life, she had hoped to be well taken care of, as were the women in the court she had envied in the past. But circumstances forced her to take on the total support of her three children. And once again she is in a position of tremendous responsibility, for she runs a major corporation, with many employees dependent on her fashion judgment. At least responsibility and the pressures it brings are familiar to her. In the past life she described, however, she took risks with her personal feelings, allowing them to take precedence over her sense of duty. In this life, Laura is forced to take risks, but only those consistent with the level of responsibility she has accepted in her public life.

Since her husband has once again betrayed her, the first feelings that occurred to her were to get even, yet she is clearly unwilling to repeat the same patterns over and over again. If she forgives her husband, perhaps Laura will free herself to achieve the ultimate level of responsibility and fame that is indicated in her chart.

In my last conversation with Laura, she said, "At least I know not to grieve so much, because it is clear that we never lose anyone from our lives. It makes things very simple. I want to develop only good relationships, because it is no good having to pay off karmic debts the hard way and having to repeat difficult relationships." As Laura takes steps to broaden her career scope, she also gives permission to her husband and to her children to take the positive kinds of risks that will give them a sense of freedom as well. Laura has just enlarged her company to include an office in the Far East. She is finally allowing herself to travel and see the world and to accept an even higher level of responsibility for her family and her career.

PAST-LIFE BOREDOM

Patricia told an amazing story of escape from what appeared to be sure death and of a tragedy that could have tempted her to give up on life. Patricia was given a project that connected her with the government of a very remote island. Her husband was able to work in his own business, and together they moved to the island community for two years. While her sister was visiting from the United States, the three of them drove to a special spot on the island, high on a cliff overlooking a spectacular view, although they knew this spot was dangerous because of the high waves that sometimes swept up over the rocks. Patricia was standing with her husband near the edge of the cliff. As she turned to walk back to her sister, a huge wave swept up over the rock where she had been standing with her husband. She turned to look over her shoulder and saw that her husband was gone. In the next second, another wave swept up, taking her backward over the cliff and far out to sea. Caught in a very strong undertow, she did the only thing she could. She held her breath and let herself be carried in this fierce maelstrom of water.

As she related this in her regression session, she said, "I know I'm going to die, and that's okay. Suddenly, when my lungs are about to burst and I have no strength left, I feel a hand that's about the size of my body, or bigger, come from underneath me and lift me above and on top of the water. It seems to keep me there long enough so that I *can* begin to breathe on my own. I can only say it is like the hand of God. I don't realize what it feels like until later on. I just know that I am suddenly above the water. I am not lifting myself, and finally I'm able to begin treading water. I'm above the force that was pulling me down.

"I'm about a quarter of a mile out to sea when this hand lifts me to the surface. Then I can rest and get into an upright position. Since I had training as a lifeguard, I know certain survival techniques. It is important to tread water as long as you can. But I realize that there is quite a current where I am. I am just outside the reef that surrounds the island. Boats cannot come inside the reef, except in certain places. I can barely see the cliff where we had stood. I have very poor vision—I'm nearly blind—and my contacts are somewhere up on that rock. I don't know whether I actually see my sister or just imagine her still standing alone on that cliff. And I'm not sure I really hear her voice saying that help is coming. I keep treading water, knowing that if I don't, I will be pushed further out to sea, and then I will really be lost. The island is very small, and I keep using that cliff as a point of reference so that my sister can see me, and so they can find me.

"This goes on for what seems an eternity, and I just keep having to decide whether I am going to keep on treading water or not make the effort. At one point, I become very angry because I am very tired. I'm angry at Peter, my husband, for not doing anything about it. He's not coming to rescue me. I'm enraged at him, and then in a few minutes, I know he is not coming because he is dead. It dawned on me just like that."

Patricia paused for a moment, and I asked her if she needed to cry. She said, "I've cried so much that I have no tears left now." She continued, "The other image that keeps coming to me is that of John F. Kennedy swimming all night in the South Pacific. (I had read his biography.) He swam for twelve hours or so when his boat went down. That's how he injured his back. Now I know firsthand that a person can continue dealing with the water. I can tell that there is some action where my sister is standing. A person jumps into the water with a surfboard and paddles out to me. I have been wondering why no one had come to me, but I also know my sister can't leave the rocks to get help. It is a very isolated place. She must stand there and wait for someone to come along so she can call for help. I also know it is very dangerous, and maybe impossible, to get to me. I expect it will be a Coast Guard boat that saves me, but I know it will take a long time, because someone will have to go all the way through the jungle to call them before they can come around to pick me up.

"The man who comes out on a surfboard is an islander. This is really a very heroic thing for him to do, because the islanders don't swim. They will not go out in the open ocean, even in boats. He is really putting his own life in danger. And he loses his life jacket diving into the ocean because of the force of the water. When he comes, I hang on to his surfboard and then I get seasick. It's funny. I don't get seasick while I'm swimming, but during the time I wait for the Coast Guard boat to arrive, I'm seasick the whole time, about half an hour. I'm able to hang on to his surfboard, and I don't have to keep treading water during that time. Once on dry land, I continue to be seasick while we go to the hospital, which takes about another half an hour."

Patricia described the fears she had while she was in the water. It has been about three and a half hours. "The waves have been about fifteen feet high, so I'm not just battling the current, I'm forever being deluged. I'm feeling the tension in my back. But the real problem is that my back has been bleeding, and I've worried about sharks for some time. Finally the bleeding stops. I am having to control any tendency to panic because I know that's the worst thing you can do. I have only one basic underlying thought: 'Do you choose to live through this?' Faced with that decision, I stay very cool. When my sister comes to the hospital, I take one look at her face and know that Peter is dead. I see my sister's agony in the hospital, and I cry as much for her pain as for my own. I've cried about that for eight and a half years. However, I know that if I begin to grieve for Peter at that moment, I won't make it. I need every bit of strength to survive."

When I asked Patricia about Peter's death, she replied, "My instinct is that he drowned immediately." After reviewing this excruciatingly painful time in her life, Patricia described her early life as being somewhat drab; everything seemed to be shades of gray. She also knew she couldn't see very well. She had been born with fifteen more blind spots than most people, and everything she saw was just a blur. Describing her birth, she said, "I'm watching. I'm not feeling like I'm supposed to do anything; I'm just looking on. Bewilderment is the word I would use. There's nothing threatening about being born, but I know I'm supposed to do something out there, and if I just knew what it was. . . . Why doesn't someone come up and tell me what it is? I have no way to interpret the data, because there's nothing to interpret. I just go along for the ride. I'm not reluctant, but I'm going to be pushed. I'm feeling a hand again, behind my back, like, 'Well, come on!' It's a very gentle hand. When I come out, the impression I get is light. Everything is shadowy. What comes into focus are doctors with masks. They are being perfunctory. There's no emotion, and there's no strong reaction from anyone. My mother is not even looking at me. She's just glad it's over with. My sense is that my father is out there in the waiting room. He seems worried. I feel, 'Well, this is okay, and what isn't there is okay, too.' It doesn't occur to me to be upset over any lack. I don't even know anything is missing. My birth survival issue seems to be, I'm the most curious of all to see what I'll do next."

Patricia then gave a perfect example of how Uranian energy manifests itself. She described the impulses that periodically led to adventures in her life. "I have always found myself far more interesting than the world. I get these flashes; a switch goes on, and I do what I feel led to do. I never know where these flashes or impulses come from. For instance, I used to participate in science fairs and thought about being a doctor, but then I entered a Miss America beauty pageant. I have no idea where that impulse came from. Having observed these impulses all my life, I just know that all of a sudden, something becomes a dead certainty. That's where my curiosity comes from. Until that switch goes on, I'm stuck in these in-between places! I still wait for that switch to go on, and I don't like the in-between states where nothing is happening. I have such continual frustration with people and places that I am just ready to exit the scene. I don't have a problem with that thought. What I would like is to find something interesting to do while I'm waiting for that switch to go on. To this very day, there is nothing that can substitute for the aliveness that suddenly happens when the switch goes on."

Patricia had described not only the boredom that accompanies the aspect of Saturn shadowing Uranus (those unending waiting periods) but also what I term the suicidal complex . . . "Please just stop the world and let me off." This comes from having lived a former life where the intellectual and spiritual level was so high that it was like breathing rarefied air, a life where one could travel at the speed of light and sound. So the boredom that sets in on the earth plane (described by Saturn) is almost intolerable. One has a tremendous desire to live, once again, where all higher perspectives and desires can be quickly manifested in the outer conditions of life. Uranus indicates leanings toward science, but in all cases, it describes brilliance of intellect that may set an individual apart from other less adventurous souls. It certainly describes a person who is a risk taker. In this earth-plane existence, however, there may be some karmic situation that prevents the "switch" from going on. Some grounding may be necessary to balance the individual energy and hold him to a slower level of existence. It may be that external blocks are necessary to prevent the person from running away prematurely, thereby missing his destiny because of lack of synchronicity with the earth plane. Certainly some guilt must be resolved.

Patricia continued with her view of herself in another existence.

"Now the scene I see is in Atlantis. I am exceedingly brilliant. I'm a philosophy teacher by the age of ten. I'm nothing but a super-brain. I try to break out and explore other aspects of my life, but by the age of twenty-five or thirty, I am tired of that level of existence but unable to change or break the mold. I am too polarized on a mental level. So I go off to live on an island until the destruction of civilization is complete. I don't live to be more than about thirty-three in that life."

When I asked Patricia to describe her view of Atlantis, she said, "My life is a very ivory tower sort of existence. My home feels like a university. It literally looks like a blazing white building with a tower, where I live. I'm female and blond. I'm very attractive. I think my mother has died in childbirth, from the baby born just after my birth. I have a father and four siblings, but I have been removed from their presence early in life. My siblings are bright, but not genius level. One of my brothers is a late bloomer in that life. He's the same brother in this life, and once again, he's the same late bloomer. Of course there's some resentment on the part of my brothers because I get a lot of attention. The role I have is not a female role, even in that society.

"My brain is like a computer, or I wouldn't be elevated to the role I have at the university. It doesn't occur to me until I'm in my mid-twenties that there is anything lacking in my life. I'm so intellectual that

I have no one to talk to. There's a terrible lack of stimulation."

Referring to what Patricia had said about her early childhood in this life, I commented, "You see how far back the boredom set in." Patricia had seen her childhood as nothing but a series of grays, shadowy and not very stimulating. She had also talked about her poor vision. She commented many times that she was just not interested in what was going on outside her in the world. I suggested that nothing in her outside world was exciting enough to make her come out of herself and look around. Her lack of interest kept her looking within. Could it be that her blindness was a result of her disinterest in exterior events and people, or just the other way around? It appeared that the beginnings of the condition existed in Atlantis, when she couldn't easily relate to the people around her because of her brilliance.

I asked Patricia to describe in more detail what her responsibilities were in connection with the university in Atlantis. She said, "I teach and I write. But beyond a certain point, my work doesn't seem to have any effect. Early on, my bent is toward the mathematical and scientific fields. It's like quantum physics somehow combined with the concepts of the Tao, so my work becomes very philosophical. There's no one else who can go into the esoteric realms, so I'm there by myself. I'm lonely because I have no one to talk to. I become a resource they can't use anymore, so I take a boat to a nearby island. I live

among the native villagers for about two years, until
the destruction of Atlantis.

"I see another life, but this time the colors are different. (I find it interesting that Atlantis was all
white.) This life is in Italy. I'm not only intellectually
bright, but I write poetry, design, and draw as well. It
is clear that this is Florence. There is more of a tapes-
try of colors, very Renaissance. Until I'm of mar-
riageable age, I'm encouraged to be involved in all
kinds of artistic activities. Then all of a sudden, it
stops. I'm not supposed to do anything anymore. I
am supposed to be married and just sit around. I
have a father and brothers. It is almost like a court
family, but more like the third or fourth tier from the
top. The name of the family may have carried down
to the present day. I see a huge villa with courtyards
and gardens. I'm beautifully dressed, with jewels
and ornaments.

"My sense is that my father tells me I'm to be married, with no forewarning. I don't have children, so I
have to sit around where everyone is weaving and
spinning and sewing. This is being female, and I'm
very bored. I'm frustrated about what to do with my
creative energy, so I try to read my stories and get the
people around me involved, but no one is interested.
There's actually a lot of warmth within the family.
Once again, I have no mother, but there is a second
wife for my father. I don't seem to have any emotional involvement with my husband. He seems to
be almost effeminate, so there's probably not a lot of
sexuality in the marriage. The turning point in my

life comes when my father tells me I'm to be married. All my free activities must cease. I die of suffocation, actually boredom, at thirty-five."

As I requested, Patricia looked at the people in that life to see if anyone came back with her into the present time. She said, "My mother, who died in that lifetime, is my sister now. We are extremely close." When I asked Patricia if she had ever had a lifetime that was exciting, she replied, "There is one lifetime where I'm a shrouded old woman, an old crone, somewhere near Ireland or Scotland. I'm standing in the middle of the woods, wearing grayish clothes. The word that comes to me is wisdom. Someone is stirring a pot. . . . I must be a witch. It's like a cartoon. The woman standing with me is like an assistant. She is relatively young, and she's stirring a pot. She's brewing something. It's late fall or spring, in the afternoon, and it's very pleasant. This is not actually an exciting life, but I have the wisdom to know it's ir-relevant. I feel very wise and contented. The difference is that I'm not looking for anything in that life, so there are no disappointments. People come to see me, and I'm respected and looked up to." After a pause, Patricia said, "My assistant in that life is my sister again." Then I asked Patricia if there was an essence in that life that she could bring into this life. She replied, "I want to invite the energy of the old woman into my life now."

I felt at the end of Patricia's session that she had touched on the true essence of Uranus in an astrologi-cal chart. Her description of her life as a wise old

woman showed that when Uranian energy is released into activities consistent with enlightenment,
boredom ceases even though outer conditions may
seem ordinary. Uranian energy can tap higher levels
of awareness and intuition that can bring light (like
electricity) to mankind. With Saturn blocks, it appears that one returns to the earth plane to integrate
that high awareness with practical everyday living,
without being pulled down into materiality. When
the feet are firmly planted on earth, the mind is free
to soar into the higher realms of inspiration.

In Patricia's case, the ability to act as an inspiration
to others may be expressed later in life. Although Patricia didn't indicate having a heavy karmic situation to resolve with her mother, she did reveal a lack
of mothering in her past lives. It would seem that she
was deprived of nurturing on a very deep level,
reaching way back and continuing into the present.
Patricia might pick career situations that would represent a technical level of responsibility but might
not propel her into the spotlight that would bring
fame. She may unconsciously avoid peaks of excitement and honor because of the memory of loneliness
in the past. For Patricia, different kinds of risks may
be necessary to tap the true healing ability she recognized from her life as the old woman. It would seem
that she came back to be a beacon for mankind, perhaps on a wider scale than in her past life.

For both Laura and Patricia, the willingness to put
themselves in a position where they can exhibit their
own levels of enlightenment seems necessary once

again. For Laura, it means learning to deal with the danger of risk, whereas for Patricia, it means dealing with a sense of isolation and loneliness yet recognizing her connection to the universe. Both Laura and Patricia have the potential to ignite others, lighting the way for all they touch through their own special kind of genius and inspiration.

A different kind of excitement can come when an individual begins to walk to the beat of a different drummer and can work through the "scare" of being somehow set apart from people in ordinary walks of life. Extraordinary people, like Einstein or Mother Theresa, may have had to conquer a sense of isolation or quell fears that their families or friends may not have known. But the willingness to pursue their own path must have brought a special sense of fulfillment, perhaps unknown to less inspired mortals.

CHAPTER 10

Change of race
from life to life.

A soul may have to experience all races and cultures if that is what is needed for the remedy, growth, or balance of the soul qualities. Allowing oneself to have prejudice, or to scoff at minority groups, may set up a future lifetime where the scoffer comes back as a member of the race or group in question. If an individual is critical or feels superior, he or she creates the basis for a boomerang situation in a future life. He may have to walk in the shoes of the person he criticized to know what it is like, for all the scales eventually have to be balanced.

When Brian did his first regression session with me, he was very resistant to answering my questions. He didn't want to follow my usual method of getting back to a past life. During his first session, however, he was able to review important issues from his childhood. Then he stopped me from going further. Brian is an extremely intelligent man, successful as a top executive in his field. He had undergone therapy and decided that my techniques are too simplistic to accomplish very much. He was very bored with the procedure and didn't really think he

Jeanne Avery

needed to continue. He stopped our session and waved me away, indicating that he had enough for one day.

Shortly after our meeting, however, Brian had a major upset in his life. His wife left him for another man. Although he suspected that she might be having an affair, he was wise enough to hope that she would be open about her needs and that she would maintain a respectful honesty. In an amazingly understanding way, he felt that if it was just a fling she needed, he hoped she would just get it out of her system, but would keep their marriage intact. What he could not tolerate was public embarrassment and lies on her part. But Sarah didn't seem to give him the same respect. She would humiliate him in front of friends by going off with the other man for hours at a time when they were at a social function. Brian discovered that instead of going on vacation by herself, to think things over, Sarah had been with the other man. He filed for a divorce.

Although he was in pain over the separation, he also knew that some burdens had been lifted from his shoulders. His twelve-year relationship with Sarah was never peaceful. She constantly argued with him and seemed to resent his authority. He said she would ask for his help and advice, then she would do just the opposite of what he suggested. He felt a strong underlying competition from her. The separation was not easy for either one of them. They had a young daughter's welfare to consider, and in addition to living together, they also worked together in the entertainment field. Sarah, in particular, felt very torn over the separation. Her coworkers reported her inability to work efficiently. She spent many hours talking to friends and shedding copious tears.

As soon as the divorce was final, Sarah married the man she had been seeing during the last stage of their marriage. As time went on, Brian began to meet, and date, very attractive young women. He seemed determined to remarry quickly, or at least to have someone steady in his life. It was not long before Brian met an attractive young lady named Jaclyn. He fell madly in love. He was sure he had known her in a past life.

Brian was eager to undertake another regression session with me. Even though he had stopped me before he revealed a past life in our previous session, he now wanted to see where he might have known Jaclyn. As I was once again attempting to encourage Brian to relinquish his control, and follow my simple instructions, he became very insistent. He said, "Jeanne, I'm getting very angry. I'm almost as frustrated and angry as when I was on that boat!"

Suddenly Brian was very quiet. He began to tell me, in a very different, very soft voice what he was seeing. He described a village in Africa. It was a peaceful village, a farming community, and he was the second son of the chieftain. His older brother was very jealous of him, as Brian was clearly the more capable of the two boys. Brian was only about twelve years old, but was wiser than his young years might indicate. The older brother created terrible problems for Brian due to jealousy and feelings of inadequacy.

Then a terrifying thing happened to their peaceful village. A large group of white men with guns came into their midst. Brian's whole family, including his older brother, was killed. Brian was captured and, along with the survivors of the village, was put into chains. The invaders forced the people to march over rough territory with no food and water. They were herded toward the sea. Eventually the chained people reached the coast and were put into a boat that was already crowded with inhabitants of several other villages.

The sea voyage was horrendous. Everyone was seasick, ill with dysentery, and very frightened. The stench of body sweat, vomit, excrement, fear, and death was almost unbearable. The Africans were taken to Haiti, where the dead were pulled off the ship and the living were paraded before the people of this strange land. The proud Africans were being sold as slaves.

When the ship reached Haiti, Brian was so weak, he was very close to death. As he collapsed on the dock, a young girl and her father bent over him. The girl's father had promised to buy a personal slave for her, and the girl selected Brian as her choice. The father argued that this boy was so weak he could do no work, and urged his daughter to select someone else. The pretty blond girl insisted that this boy was the one she wanted, and the father finally relented. Brian knew, immediately, that the girl was Jaclyn.

Brian was barely conscious, but he realized that he was taken to the main house of a plantation and then to the girl's room. He was placed on a pallet on the floor, close to the girl's bed. Jaclyn and her mammy began to feed him and gently nurse him back to health. It took many months for him to recover, and he continued to live in her room, along with the mammy. Eventually he was too old to stay there and, for propriety's sake, went to live in the slave quarters. But he and Jaclyn remained friends for the rest of their lives. They were almost inseparable. Unfortunately, the two young people did not live past their teen years.

When Brian opened his eyes after the session, I could see a new demeanor, a new bearing, and a softening of his personality. When he was ready to respond, I asked him if he knew any of the people from that life in his present existence. He was wide-eyed as he said, "Sarah, my ex-wife, was my older brother. No wonder we've had so many problems in this life." Brian informed me that the most amazing part of the session, for him, was the smell of that boat. The putrid aroma was the first thing that broke through into his consciousness.

A few weeks later, Brian called to tell me the sequel to his regression session. In a phone conversation with his ex-wife, Sarah, he shared his experience and told her what he had envisioned about their past relationship. Brian was brief in his description of her reaction but, a short time after that conversation, she reported to him that she stopped crying after learning of their past association. Brian said they have not had a single argument since then.

As Brian became more acquainted with Jaclyn, she shared a dream with him. In that dream she saw a past-life relationship with him. That dream took place long before they actually met, but Jaclyn "recognized" Brian as the person in her dream as soon as she saw him. Brian did not tell Jaclyn the details of his memory of their past association, since Jaclyn planned to do a regression session with me as soon as possible.

When we were working together, Jaclyn brought out many details that she had not recalled previously. I was not surprised that those details dovetailed, exactly, with what Brian had uncovered in his session. The events of the life Brian and Jaclyn shared in Haiti is historically accurate, but neither Jaclyn nor Brian had actual knowledge of the historical events in Haiti at that time period. I, having visited Haiti, was aware of the significance of their memories.

Both Brian and Jaclyn described a period of Haitian history when Toussaint L'Ouverture, Pierre Dominique, and Jean Jacques Dessalines led a slave uprising in Haiti in 1794. In that successful uprising, five hundred thousand blacks and mulattoes armed themselves against forty thousand white Haitian plantation owners and residents. Brian saw himself as a leader of the slaves on the plantation where he lived, the plantation owned by Jaclyn's father. He envisioned himself as a young man, hardly more than a teenager, and thought he might have been

Toussaint L'Ouverture. However, L'Ouverture was a fifty-one-year-old military man, who was eventually sent to France by General Leclerc. L'Ouverture was said to be one of Pauline Bonaparte's lovers, and although the slaves won the uprising, L'Ouverture died in prison in France after General Leclerc brought new French troops to Haiti in 1802. Brian remembered himself as an important leader in that uprising but the youngest of the three leaders, Henri Christophe, was twenty-seven years old. Whether Brian was actually one of the three major leaders, or not, had little to do with the memories of that life. He saw his courage, his ability to fight for what was right, and knew that his heart was still with the beautiful girl who had saved his life. It seemed impossible that the past-life relationship with Jaclyn could come to fruition in that lifetime due to their racial differences. However, Brian still knew himself to be a prince, a son of a former chieftain from Africa. He tried to protect Jaclyn from harm during the ensuing battles.

Jaclyn saw Brian stealthily entering the boundaries of the plantation at night, with torches dimly lighting the scene. He was there to find Jaclyn and to persuade her to come away with him to safety. However, Jaclyn's father discovered them together, and raised a gun to shoot Brian. Jaclyn evidently threw herself between her father and Brian and was killed. Jaclyn's father was shot by one of Brian's compatriots, and Brian was killed by someone who was there to protect Jaclyn and her father. However, their ill-fated love and deep caring from a lifetime in Haiti brought them together again in the present time.

It was odd that Brian described a time in history that I knew so well. I had already conducted a regression session with a man who was separated from his wife. He was in the process of getting a divorce and was going to Haiti for the final decree. Glen recently met a woman he was interested in and had persuaded her to travel to Haiti with him on his "divorce trip." Since Glen had been to see me for a session, he suggested that Barbara also make an appointment for a regression. He thought they might have been together in a past existence. In light of later events, one significant factor emerged when Glen was reviewing his childhood. He was surrounded by black musicians as a young boy, because his father invited his friends to their home for "jam" sessions. As Glen was going to sleep, he would hear the music night after night, and was often tucked into bed by one of his father's friends. He was looking forward to visiting Haiti, where extraordinary artists painted wonderful primitive canvases. He was curious to see what the music might be like. One of the things that stuck out in my mind as Barbara was describing her present-life relationship with Glen was that he had two irritating habits. Whenever they entered a cab with a driver from Haiti, Glen carried on a lengthy conversation with the driver instead of with Barbara. There were times when Barbara might have fairly urgent things to discuss with him, but she could not get his attention if he was talking to a driver. He also stopped people on the street to have a conversation.

Glen's most irritating habit was of giving himself a nickname. It had manifested when he went to the jewelry district and ordered a pendant to be crafted in silver with a thunderbolt on one side. He wore it around his neck all the time. On the other side of the pendant was the inscription "Son of Thunder," his nickname for himself. Although Barbara realized that Glen was getting out of a very restrictive marriage and obviously needed to let his free spirit loose in any way possible, his nickname seemed a bit strange and grandiose. She decided to ignore her irritations and enjoy their times together.

Both sessions were enlightening and helpful for Barbara and Glen. However, nothing significant emerged about a past-life association. I suggested that while they were away, they might review other lives between themselves. When they returned from Haiti, Barbara called to tell me what had transpired. She said, "I can hardly believe that it happened."

At the time of their trip, one special hotel was newly opened. It had a reputation of great extravagance and luxury, and Glen tried to get reservations at L'Habitation Leclerc. The hotel had been the former home of General Charles Victor Emmanuel Leclerc and his wife, Pauline Bonaparte, the sister of the French emperor Napoleon. General Leclerc had been sent by Napoleon to Haiti, along with twenty-five thousand soldiers, to reverse the slave rebellion and revoke the emancipation decree of 1794. Since Barbara was interested in the history of the beautiful mansion, she described her determination to obtain a copy of a booklet published by the hotel that described the events that took place during the occupation of the Leclercs.

Glen and Barbara were able to dine at the hotel and visit the popular discotheque located there. Glen's pretense of familiarity with the place was an additional irritating factor to Barbara, but she ignored his comments such as, "That tree wasn't there before. The stairs seemed steeper in my other life." Throughout the whole trip, Glen discussed his familiarity with the Haitian terrain. Barbara said, "I'm afraid I dismissed much of it as mere fantasy, and I was slightly bored with his running commentary." When the evening at L'Habitation Leclerc was over, Barbara awakened a sleepy desk clerk and insisted that he find a copy of the brochure she wanted to read. When she and Glen arrived back in their room, she began reading about the extravagant parties that took place, and discovered that Pauline Bonaparte had many, many lovers. Her promiscuity was evidently well-known at the time.

Barbara said she found it unusual that she would be interested in this material at all, yet she described tearing off page by page of the stapled booklet and handing them over to Glen to read for himself. She said, "I was suddenly almost paralyzed by what I saw. The brochure described Pauline Bonaparte's relationship with Toussaint L'Ouverture. The booklet gave his name and then, in parentheses, it said, 'Son of Thunder.' I couldn't believe what I was reading. Glen and I talked about his memories of the mansion, and this time I paid attention. He had not known his formal name, but the nickname stuck in his subconscious very clearly. No wonder he wanted to go to Haiti for his divorce. He was able to fill in many details about a life as L'Ouverture. Before we left Haiti, he found a book about L'Ouverture's life written in French. But Glen's French was superb, and he read the book all the way home on the plane. According to what I've learned through my own research, Glen's memories of the events dovetailed exactly with the documented history of that time. I'm sure he was Toussaint L'Ouverture in a Haitian lifetime."

I remembered, very clearly, what Glen had described when he went to a past life. He saw himself leading a military coup and being successful. He then saw that he was given a hero's parade through a town and later went across a body of water to France, where he had a relationship with a very prominent woman. He described himself as being very dark, but didn't specify that he was black. He saw that at a later time he was imprisoned. He thought he was released and went back to an island in the Caribbean. Those sketchy memories were historically accurate, except for the return trip to Haiti. It is my understanding that he died in prison. Even though his capsulized version of the rest of L'Ouverture's life after the slave uprising was lacking in some details, I, too, was quite sure he was describing himself as Toussaint L'Ouverture of Haiti.

Many years ago, a beautiful young black girl came to see me for a regression session. She was poised, elegant, intelligent, and quite self-assured. It was immediately apparent, from her review of her present life, that she had a mission in her young life. She was a perfect representative of an accomplished young black woman, yet she had already encountered terrible racial prejudice in her life. She was determined to fight for the rights of black women everywhere.

As we prepared to go to her past life, Caroline squirmed in her seat and seemed puzzled at what she was seeing. Finally, she described the scene before her eyes. She said, "I'm white! It appears that I live on a southern plantation and am the spoiled darling daughter of a wealthy landowner. I'm the apple of my father's eyes." With very little help from me, Caroline realized that she had been arrogant, to an extreme, in her dealings with the black people who worked the plantation. She said, "I even treat my personal slave with the most horrible disdain for her welfare. I don't seem to care whether she is healthy or sick, tired or hungry. I expect her to be there to do my bidding whenever I want even the smallest things. I'm horrified to see my attitude toward these people." Before Caroline finished her session, it was clear that her message to black women would be different now. The new perspective on her present life, as viewed from the past racially biased viewpoint, gave her a totally new approach to the issue of discrimination. Caroline decided to expand her goals to fight for rights across the lines of gender and race.

When Caroline reviewed her present relationship with a young black man named Bill, she recognized him as her childhood friend in the southern life. As Caroline grew older and began to prepare for her debut into society, she abandoned the friendship because of the difference in the color of their skin. She commented, "Now I understand my resistance to making future plans with Bill in the present time. I have a lot of guilt that has kept big walls between us. I will ask for his forgiveness, and I hope he will accept my recounting of this amazing revelation. Perhaps Bill will come for his own regression session. He is the type of person who can help me in my mission, but he still has the attitude I had before I started this process. I'm not sure he could understand unless he sees the situation for himself. I owe him so much. I must have hurt him deeply by my behavior then." I suggested that Caroline put Bill in front of her, in her mind's eye, and talk to him. She tearfully apologized for her shallow behavior toward someone who genuinely was her friend in the past. She said, "I think this might pave the way for a deeper communication between us. I now know it has been my resistance that kept the walls up between us."

CHAPTER 11

How to conduct self-regression; rectifying past mistakes.

Every problem has its roots in the past, and it follows that we are the authors of our scripts in the theater of our present lives. From the perspective of present-day circumstances, it is easy to overlook cause and effect, and the results of acts we commit. We may not be aware that every tiny action or choice in life is like planting a seed for the future. The plant will grow in exact proportion to the seed that is planted. However, from a past-life point of view, we cannot help but see the patterns that have set in motion the conditions and relationships we face in the here and now. So the first step to take, when we are forced to change present-day interactions and events, is to acknowledge that no one but ourselves can be responsible for the present conditions of our lives. That may be a difficult step to take, but nothing is resolved if we blame our parents, or life, or external conditions. The people around us are merely other actors, performing their roles according to their own scripts and life dramas. They are no more or no less than mirrors that enable us to see our true reflection.

The intricate interweaving and deciphering of relationships can be one of the most fascinating subjects for review in one's whole life. If things are out of balance, and events seem out of our control in spite of good intentions, then it's time to ask specific questions on the level of our higher consciousness. That lack of balance can produce enough pain to create a need for an adjustment, like a chiropractor adjusting the spine. That may be the perfect moment to begin asking questions of oneself, such as: "Where did such a condition have its beginning? Where might I have known this person before? What could our relationship have been in the past? How was it resolved? What are we to learn from each other?"

In a regression session, a person learns how to ask such questions of himself and, most importantly, listen for the answers. In essence, self-regression is the process of developing the ability to dialogue with the subconscious mind. Sustaining that dialogue and retrieving information from the subconscious storehouse can be developed, with time and practice, like learning how to flex unused muscles in a gym. The more the exercise, the easier are the desired results. When a person becomes proficient in this technique, he or she can have access to that part of the mind whenever there is a need for more information about himself, other people, or life around him.

I vividly recall the way in which one important lifetime emerged into my consciousness. I had undergone only one formal regression session many years prior to the incident, but since that first experience, I had recalled many lifetimes on my own. Therefore, I was willing to trust any thoughts or fantasy that came to my mind in regard to past life situations. At the least I was willing to accept information coming to mind to see if it seemed relevant or valid in my present life.

I was conducting a workshop and giving lectures in Italy one summer. Since I had a weekend break, I decided to visit Florence. As I was driving toward the city in broad daylight, I had an unexpected vision. I saw the figure of a man floating in the sky ahead of me. He appeared to be around thirty or thirty-five years old, and was dressed in what seemed to be academic attire. He was wearing a robe and a flat-topped hat with a tassel to one side. My immediate impression was that I had lived in Florence as a man during the time of the Renaissance. Fortunately, I wasn't startled, and the vision disappeared as rapidly as it appeared. I thought to myself, "That was one of the very few lifetimes I lived in a male body. I've almost always been a woman."

Another thought came to mind. With the identification of myself as a scholarly man in a former time, I could more fully understand my lifelong interest in academia. I was an eager student from early childhood, majoring in mathematics and Latin in preparation for college. I always achieved top grades and won many honors in school. I was known as a brain in high school, but I really wanted to be pretty and popular. Upon graduation I was awarded an academic scholarship to a major university. However, I did not pursue that facet of my life, choosing to work in the theater instead. I always continued to read a great deal, and I quietly furthered my education by studying a variety of subjects on my own initiative.

After I arrived in Florence and walked through the streets, I fell in love with the city. I only wished I could find a way to live there permanently. I was especially curious to visit the de Medici Palace. As I entered the lovely gardens, chills ran up and down my spine. It all seemed very familiar. I could even sense that I had lived on these very grounds, and I felt as though I could locate the area, if not the very building, where I had spent a lot of time. I knew I was not a member of the de Medici family, but the sensation of having been a man of learning and of being sponsored by the de Medici family was very strong. The images that came into my consciousness seemed to be a restimulation of a present-life situation that had occurred only a few months prior to my trip to Italy.

When I was living in Aspen, Colorado, I met a lovely couple through mutual friends. They were on a short vacation and were returning home to a major southern city almost immediately. But we developed a strong rapport in a short period of time, which was underscored by the fact that the wife, whom I will call Eleanor, shared my birthday. Even though she was born in a different year, our life circumstances were so similar it was startling. Both Eleanor and I had been "adopted," and our adopted mothers were so alike in personality they might have been twins.

Eleanor was adopted as an infant, whereas I went

to live with a distant relative when I was only four years old. This came about in my life because a wonderful woman, the sister-in-law of a cousin to my mother, took an interest in my education. My father died when I was only two years old, and my mother was still suffering the trauma of his loss. This sincerely devoted relative convinced my mother that I should come to live with her and her husband so that I could attend school in a northern city. She felt that I needed to be in an area where I could have many cultural and scholarly advantages. Each year I would return to my home in a small, sleepy, southern town for holidays and the summer, to be with my mother and sister.

The special lady, whom I nicknamed "Missy," fell in love with me before she ever met me, and was already determined to take a hand in my upbringing before we ever set eyes on each other. We adored each other for the rest of our lives. I always felt as though I had two mothers, even though Missy was of a grandmotherly age, for I loved both of these extraordinary women with all my heart. Missy surely must have been my real mother in another life.

Eleanor's mother arranged for her adoption as soon as she was born and adored her as completely as if she had been her natural-born child. Eleanor reciprocated with deep, passionate love. Both Eleanor and I were truly devastated when our mothers died. Eleanor also graduated from high school when she was only sixteen with very high honors—almost straight A's—as had I. We were both married very young and had three children that we were completely devoted to. There were many other similarities. The major difference was that Eleanor's adopted family was extremely wealthy, whereas my "adopted" family was of comfortable, but moderate, means.

Shortly before my trip to Florence, I was lecturing in the area where Eleanor lived. She was very eager to do a regression session with me while I was nearby, in hopes that she might discover details about her true background, as her adoption records had been carefully concealed by her parents. Eleanor's husband wasn't sure that she should attempt to uncover this information about her heritage, but Eleanor was determined to find out whatever she could about her natural-birth mother. Eleanor always thought that she was Italian, although she was adopted by a Jewish family and was brought up in that faith. The regression session revealed a great deal of information about her real mother and the circumstances of her birth, even though she was only with her for a very few hours before going to be with her new family. Through that experience, Eleanor got to know her natural mother in a way she could never have expected.

When she went to a past life, she saw herself as a member of a very powerful family in Italy. Although she was reluctant to name the family, she finally confessed that she was a de Medici. Eleanor was quite astonished by her revelation and was a bit shy about claiming to be part of that powerful family. She was a woman in that life, married to the same man as she was in the present. The relationship was deep and loving both then and now.

My knowledge of the de Medici family was scant. I knew they were the most powerful banking family in Tuscany and were influential in the world of art and politics at the time of the Renaissance. I was aware that Lorenzo de Medici had committed extraordinarily brutal acts in retaliation for the murder of his brother, Guiliano, and I certainly knew that they were thought to be ruthless and corrupt in their desire for political power. But I knew few other facts or names of their political associations during their reign in Italy. I was determined to further investigate that period of history when I had some free time.

During my stay in that southern city, Eleanor was not only gracious but extended such courtesy to me that I was almost overwhelmed. She invited me to come to live with her family so that I could concentrate on finishing my second book without pressure. She showed me a wing of her home and told me that if I needed privacy, my food could be brought to the door and I would never have to leave that part of her home unless I wanted to. She assured me that she would never intrude on my writing time, even in her own home, unless I invited her to visit. I was very touched by her offer and knew she meant it very sincerely. I wanted to accept her kind offer, but I suspected that I would be unable to resist spending more time with her and her family, rather than sticking to a strict writing schedule. So I reluctantly declined her invitation.

When I was able to do a bit of research, I discovered that the de Medici family were generous benefactors to artists and great thinkers of the time. In 1428, when Giovanni de Medici, the founding father of the Florentine banking house, was at the height of influence in Tuscan society, the University of Florence began to teach Greek and Latin literature. They put special emphasis on history and its bearing on human behavior and moral values. In 1429 Giovanni de Medici died, leaving his son Cosimo as head of the Florentine banking house. Giovanni advised his son to be charitable to the poor and to belong to the popular political party. Cosimo ruled over Florence from 1429 until he was exiled in 1433, but he was recalled a year later to resume the position of ruler of Florence until his death in 1464. His family continued to dominate the city for another thirty years. During that time, there were many artisans who were supported by the family and who lived on the de Medici property. They seemed to have complete access to the palace and lived in an atmosphere that encouraged discussion and expression of all phases of life and art.

As I walked through the gardens of the palace, I felt that the physical sensation of chills down my back was a confirmation of what Eleanor had uncovered in her regression session. I sensed that, as the scholarly man, I must have been one of those people who lived on the grounds of the palace. It almost seemed too "pat" that the same kind of circumstance would reoccur in the present; that I would once again be invited to live with the former de Medicis in the present time. However, I have learned through working with other people that patterns continue to repeat almost exactly lifetime after lifetime in a very amazing way. And the events in my life had unfolded "backwards." The present-life events triggered my desire to visit Florence and the de Medici palace. Otherwise, I might not have made the trip to Florence at that moment when I had so little time. I'm not sure that I would have tuned into a sense of a lifetime spent in Florence, although I had always wanted to visit that beautiful city. At that moment in my life, I was too preoccupied with other things to be searching for a past life. So the awareness of that former existence came almost literally "out of the blue," and I was pleasantly surprised to observe how the revelation of my life in Florence gave credence to my instant "recognition" and deep feelings of friendship toward the couple I had so recently met.

I was quite content with my new awareness of a very pleasant life in Florence, and the images made sense to me. But, as it turned out, there was more about the experience of that time to be revealed. I had no additional curiosity about the man dressed in his academic robes, as to who he might have been, nor did I plan to search for more information about that lifetime. I did ask myself when and where I had developed an interest in astrology, however.

As an actress, I felt that I had achieved a certain security in my ability and I had worked hard to build a reputation within the industry. My becoming an astrologer was something that simply grew out of circumstances. I had never planned to work in this field on a professional basis. So I had some curiosity as to why my life had taken such a dramatic turn. I decided I may have been an astrologer in ancient Egypt, as an example.

One day a friend of mine gave me a book about an astrologer who lived centuries ago. I am ashamed to admit that I had never heard of Marsilio Ficino. He was a poor parish priest, philosopher, and astrologer who was born at the time of the Renaissance. He lived during the last thirty years of the reign of Cosimo de Medici. Marsilio Ficino called Cosimo de Medici "the father of my soul," so they must have been in close association. Marsilio Ficino lived through the violent political times prior to, and after, the murder of Guiliano de Medici when Lorenzo de Medici was avenging his brother's death and struggling to maintain political supremacy.

When my friend gave me a copy of the obscure book about the life of Ficino, she said to me, "I think you were this man." I thanked her profusely and having very little time to read, put the book aside. I completely ignored her comment about my possible connection with the astrologer of the fifteenth century. One day I happened to come across the volume again and picked it up out of idle curiosity. I read about three pages and froze in a state of shock. The words I read on those pages were almost exactly the phrases and words I use to describe planetary energies and how they manifest in the life of an individual. The book was like a hot potato in my hand, and I dropped it, never to read it again. To this day, I cannot locate the book when I want to investigate its contents. It is almost as if that book has a life of its own. The book appears from time to time when I am not able to read it, but I can never find it when I decide to tackle the contents seriously and objectively.

Subsequently I met a gentleman from Europe who told me he was among the more fortunate souls of the world. He had inherited enough family money to live an extremely leisurely and scholarly life. He was interested and knowledgeable about astrology and had an ongoing love relationship with an Italian astrologer. Together they planned to produce an astrological television show in Italy. They asked me to meet them because of our mutual interest in the subject. During that meeting I was asked many questions about my theories and views of astrology, and I finally realized they may have been interviewing me for some participation with the show. In a totally naive way I said, "I think I was Marsilio Ficino." The discussion and interview ended very abruptly. The gentleman's reaction was one of horror. "Don't you know he was one of the great thinkers of the Renaissance?" he said. After a moment of stunned silence, I quickly added, "Then, of course, I must be mistaken."

The moral of my story is this; it is not important to know who you *were*, but who you *are*! I cannot say, for sure, that I was the philosopher and astrologer named Marsilio Ficino. It is really unimportant to know if I was or was not that man from the time of the Renaissance. But my subconscious mind, or my cosmic mind, revealed specific information to my conscious mind to be used, at the least, as a metaphor for my current life. If I had closed the door on the sensations and information, I would miss having another dimension of comprehension about my life and work.

I have always detested the dirty tricks that seem to accompany political activity, whether that activity is on a governmental level or is related to business, or even socially. Ficino wrote many letters to a variety of men of the time who were struggling to keep a balance between the swirling maelstrom of revenge for deeds done to them and their conscience, which told them to adhere to their inner convictions and sense of moral ethics rather than to give in to the cruelty and avarice of the times. He most often used astrological terminology and higher spiritual concepts to illustrate his point.

When an individual is attempting to do a self-regression, there is a temptation to deny, rather than claim, any association with someone who had been famous (or infamous) in a past life. Many people say, "Everyone was a king or queen in a past life." But it is simply not true. Each life, whether the person was in a highborn position or a lowly position, has a message for the present existence. The importance of looking within is to find the message inside the fortune cookie of our subconscious minds.

* * *

There are many techniques one can use to tap the subconscious in order to retrieve the information stored within. The common method of regression is to utilize hypnosis. Another interesting method may come through acupuncture, acupressure, or some similar technique. I experienced a flashback to a significant past life when I was undergoing a therapy session using Wilhelm Reich's technique of deep muscle pressure. My friend and therapist, psychiatrist Dr. Richard Blasband, had no idea I was going to a past-life situation until our session was completed. Nor was that my intention. But I saw vivid details of a scene that I was later able to confirm by going to the location I viewed in that session. The jail cell I saw later on was exactly as I had pictured it in my work with Dr. Blasband, down to the absolute last detail of the cobblestone walkway underneath the small barred window. Coincidentally, one of my greatest horrors as a child was to think of someone being locked up or confined against his or her will.

When I work with a client, with the express purpose of going to a past life through the process of regression, I do not use hypnosis or physical methods. Everyone I've worked with has been able to tap into hitherto hidden information in a completely natural state of awareness. The sessions usually last three hours and reveal enough information to reach a decisive point of clarification about present-day conditions. The aimed for focus is the one that will clarify present-life relationships and patterns. Everyone reaches what I call the dropped stitch on the thread of consciousness. Naturally, one can do many sessions and continue with the unraveling process, but once the key to unblocking the hidden matters becomes clear, a person may discover that the information reveals itself at exactly the right and appropriate time in life.

I conduct sessions without using hypnosis because each person has the ability to gain information naturally. It is my goal to show an individual how self-reliant he or she can be. The more a person trusts his or her own ability to find answers within, the less dependent that person becomes on someone else. If one can learn to reveal this information naturally, and resolve his own problems, true freedom of spirit has a chance to reign supreme.

There is no need to set the conscious mind aside. The conscious part of the intellect plays a valuable part in assessing the information that is revealed and therefore should not be set aside. The end result brings very deep, new psychological awareness, not just momentary, and perhaps titillating examination of past-life adventures. In fact, I feel a regression session is viable only if it is conducted with the serious intent of examining deep-seated patterns and relationships. The purpose is to re-create a better quality of life as the result of improved relationships.

It is important not to be concerned about whether the information that comes forth in these sessions is accurate. If it is part of a person's fantasy, it belongs to him and therefore is valid psychologically. In the case of people who revealed past lives that could be confirmed historically, the accuracy of minute details is equally unimportant. Whatever emerges from a person's subconscious may be his or her special perception of what really happened. Memories can be flawed as time elapses, even in the present life, but characterization of people and events, gained in a regression session, explains present-day situations in a way that nothing can else can accomplish with such clarity. It is important for the success of the regression not to put oneself under pressure to be right or correct in the details. Those details can emerge as time goes by, clarifying and augmenting the pictures that come to mind. What is important about any retrieved memories is how they relate to events in the present. If any such revelation brings about new insights, it becomes a productive experience.

The Akashic Records contain information about each person's thoughts, actions, and deeds throughout all of history. Students of metaphysics are familiar with the concept that everything has been recorded, almost magnetically, in the Akashic Records. These records exist on some sphere or energy level not readily available to everyone. However, the entire history of human collective and individual activity exists there, to be tapped whenever someone finds the key that fits the lock. There are no secrets in the universe! But, mercifully, we have little access to those records until we have developed the sense of responsibility and wisdom that must go hand in hand with possession of this knowledge. We are blissfully unaware of what we may have done in the past until the time comes when we can handle that information without threat to our survival. For this protection, we can be thankful to the left brain, which allows us to accept only what we can see, touch, taste, hear, smell, and measure. Otherwise the knowledge (perhaps the same knowledge of good and evil described in the Bible) might be more than we could cope with.

At some point in our psychological/spiritual development, the "overself," or soul consciousness, causes us to become curious about unseen matters. When we have developed another level of consciousness, and want to know more about the interactions with people around us, we begin to look more deeply into the nature of things. We can develop an ability to see people and events as our mirror. New concepts about the continuation of all life, sentient or otherwise, comes with observation of patterns in nature, such as the never-ending cycle of seasons. We may learn about life through observing plants or animals. Eventually we make a correlation between what we observe in our own lives and in all manner of life around us. Our curiosity begins to take us on an inner journey that is as exciting as anything we might experience on a conscious level. Sometimes that journey begins as a result of health issues, pain, discouragement, or other very real life problems. If those problems cannot be answered by someone outside of ourselves, we are forced to fall back upon ourselves and look within. We finally learn to pay attention to outer signals that indicate a need to go within.

On our inner journey, it is the left brain that asks the practical questions, observes and assimilates knowledge. The right brain has many answers stored that come forth only in the process of listening on a higher level. Learning to have a dialogue with the subconscious is as simple as learning to ask the right questions and listening for the answers that come from within.

Some people seem to have easier access to subconscious information than others. In certain regression sessions, the information pours out. I am almost totally silent, simply listening while the individual in front of me relates his experiences. In other cases, I must work very hard to facilitate the flow of information that seems trapped or buried inside. In either case, my prime function seems to be to keep the person on the right track by asking him questions that will lead him to his own answers.

In doing a regression session alone, it is important to keep a dialogue going inside and not let the mind wander aimlessly. Sometimes it helps to ask the question of oneself out loud, not silently. Since the analytical part of the mind acts as a guardian to the door of the subconscious, it becomes the protector of the mind, doling out only what the total being can assimilate. I stress that one should trust the function of his left brain, knowing that it will release only what is appropriate at the moment. Keeping the focus on these questions will protect and guide a person to the pertinent information stored within the right brain.

The mind is like a file cabinet with a combination lock on the outside. The left brain processes the combination on that lock, which opens the door to the file cabinet. The files stored inside that cabinet are analogous to the information within the right brain, and the subconscious, intuitive part of the mind. However, imagine that the last secretary to put information into that cabinet left a mess. She put the files in scattered order and forgot to file some very important documents. In a regression session, the individual is simply looking inside to retrieve all the pieces of paper in a proper order to complete the picture. With that look, he begins to rearrange the data and locate any missing material.

Once that rearranging job is finished, he has easy access to everything in that file cabinet and can open the door whenever he wants. When he closes the door and sets the combination lock, the information is safe once again. However, since he glanced at all those odd scraps of information, he has a pretty good idea of what is contained within his family records, or his own mind. His thoughts are now uncluttered because the file cabinet is in order, and he can express much more of his mental energy in a productive way.

This leads to a new perspective that changes one's life, usually after only one session. Decisions and actions that occurred during moments of trauma, loss, or pain may cause aberrant behavior. As the new perspectives blend into outer consciousness, the patterns and data that have been rearranged in the regression session cause the person to live his life in a different manner simply because he begins to see things clearly and therefore makes different kinds of decisions.

Here's an example of how all this would work. Let's say that a child has been protected, loved, well fed, and well cared for. He is secure with his environment. One day he is taking a nap when the family dog runs out of the house and is hit by a car. Mother runs out of the house to rescue the dog. She leaves the door open so she can hear the baby, but she goes next door to see if her neighbor will take the dog to a veterinarian. Meanwhile, the baby, perhaps sensing something traumatic, awakens early. He cries, to alert Mother that she is needed, but she doesn't respond as she usually does. He cries a little louder, but she doesn't come. Finally he screams, and Mother can hear him from the neighbor's house. She runs home to get him, leaving the dog in the neighbor's care, but it is too late for the child. He has now said to himself, "My mother left me! She doesn't love me! I can never trust her again." Moreover, her attitude when she picks him up is very different. He can sense the difference, but he can't read her mind. He can't say, "Mother, why didn't you come for me?" and she, being concerned about the dog, doesn't realize that the baby needs an explanation to help him feel secure once more.

The relationship between the two has changed.

The baby now sees his mother as someone he can't completely trust. She only knows that formerly he was such a good baby. Now he cries when she leaves the room for just a moment. She becomes annoyed and tells him not to be a naughty baby. The pattern that has been set in motion is very different from the pattern of the loving, trusting relationship that existed before. Now the child begins to pull away and becomes cautious about expressing open love and affection. The former easy love, trust, and companionship between the mother and child has been changed forever. Unfortunately, that sets a pattern in motion that lasts the rest of the child's life.

SELF-REGRESSION TECHNIQUES

First, there is a need for reflection and review. A regression session can put you in touch with your own records so that you can see exactly what you have written in the past. This releases you to make positive decisions about how to restore balance in your own life and in relation to other people.

Secondly, you need time for that reflection on a daily basis. Meditation is one of the most powerful tools you can use for deep, productive reflections. Meditation must be active, not passive. By that I mean it is important to meditate on something, not nothing. That something could be a seed thought repeated over and over again like a mantra. Or it might be meditation on symbols that are meaningful. Focusing on one thing over and over is like dropping water on a stone. It is a process that helps develop the ability to clear the mind. Just as with a computer, there is a blank screen in front of you. However, first you have to learn how to turn the computer on and focus on the right key to push in order to access information onto that blank screen.

Finally, you need to allow time for the results of your new decisions to manifest in your life. If you become impatient and delete what you put in your computer, write over the text with something new, or put in doubtful words that obfuscate the message you're sending to the universe, the results will be confusing. It is possible to conduct a dialogue with your higher self all by yourself. You can do it, *if* you can do it. It is a matter of asking yourself one question at a time and learning how to listen for the answer. With practice it can be easy, depending on how much you can focus your mind on the exact questions you're asking. Then it is a decision to dedicate yourself to hearing the answer.

Since I conduct regression sessions without the use of hypnosis, new information can continue to float into consciousness after a regression session is over. I stress that it is important to leave the judgmental mind aside in all regression work so that information can continue to pop into the mind as time goes on. On many occasions, a person calls to tell me amazing information that has come forth after the session is over. Working in this way is actually developing an ability to open the doors to the Akashic

Records. This can only be done by conscious, focused attention on the process.

Again, I stress that it is important not to be concerned about whether the information you receive is "accurate" or not. Fantasy belongs to each person as much as if the thoughts can be proven and verified. What is important about the process you undertake is how those past impressions relate to your life patterns and associations with those you love or hate. If any revelation can give explanation or can clarify situations in the present, it has great value in your ability to create life anew.

I use the analogy of knitting to explain the process. Imagine knitting a sweater. As you are working on the twenty-fifth row, you suddenly realize that you've dropped a stitch on the eighteenth row. Your sweater won't be a very good sweater unless you go back and pick up the stitch. It is my opinion that in traditional therapeutic practices, the work you do is similar to picking up a crochet hook and weaving that dropped stitch into the whole sweater again. It is then necessary to pull and stretch the knitting around that dropped stitch to integrate it into the weave of the sweater. Sometimes that stitch shows, and the pile isn't very smooth. It may be necessary to go back once more to pick out that stitch and try again to blend it into the whole garment more evenly.

A regression session can augment a traditional therapeutic process, because in the regression session, a person unravels each row of knitting to pick up that dropped stitch. The rows represent crisis times in life when inappropriate decisions are likely to be made. Eventually, the sweater begins to knit itself up again. By that I mean that with one or two regression sessions you allow new information to float up to the surface, filling in information about the patterns of life without any further assistance from an external source. In a regression session, I do not leave a person until he or she has reached that dropped stitch. After that type of inner work, any time spent with more traditional types of psychotherapy will be enriched and will make the therapeutic work even more effective. As the individual understands the basic formula he or she has set up for his or her life, the pieces of the puzzle will continue to fall into place, like cleaning a dusty mirror so that the reflection is clear in all its glorious detail.

First, sit erect rather than lying down. A position similar to a meditation pose not only helps you with the concentration necessary but allows energy to flow downward from a higher sphere of consciousness into the brain.

Next, close your eyes. That is helpful in blocking out the current environment and all the Pavlovian responses connected to your present condition.

Then direct yourself to review some of the hardships, pain, or traumas you've experienced in this lifetime. After you've thought through a recent difficult time from the perspective of your higher, objective mind, direct yourself to go back to an earlier moment of pain or loss. That may be physical pain or emotional pain, physical loss or emotional loss. After you've reviewed several situations, ask yourself what the connection might be between them.

A very simplistic example may be that you've just had a minor automobile accident after having had a fight with your spouse. In an earlier moment you may have fallen down and skinned your knee just after you've been angry at something your mother or father said or did. You may be able to trace those patterns quite far back. The new perspective you gain is that you better observe and acknowledge anger or frustration and take time to cool down before racing out to your automobile or before crossing streets against the light. That kind of awareness may not be very difficult to attain. But, of course, one can go much deeper.

Let's review the description of the baby, lying in the crib, wondering where Mother might be. Suppose you've merely asked yourself for a very early moment of pain or loss, and you see a small baby. You don't see anything to indicate that the moment is significant, however, and you may be ready to dismiss that image as simply your imagination. However, if you persist and ask yourself, "What am I doing in that crib?" you may get an impression that you are crying. You may then ask yourself, "What time of day or night is this?" The answer might be "Three o'clock in the afternoon." Perhaps you are stuck for the next question. Take a look around the room to observe the furniture, the color of the walls, whether there is a rug on the floor and curtains on the window. This process helps to place you in that moment and enables more insights to come to mind. You may realize that you are feeling alone or frightened, and you may realize that you know Mother is not in the house. Then you can ask yourself, "Where is she?" You might draw a blank again, but please refrain from saying to yourself, "I don't know;" you actually know everything if you persist in asking. If necessary, ask five times until you force yourself into coming up with an answer! Eventually what you realize is that mother is next door at the neighbor's house and there is some sort of an emergency. You might ask yourself what kind of emergency, although that is not so important to your sense of comfort. You can then ask if Mother is coming back soon, and if the answer is "Yes," you can convince yourself to play with the mobile above your bed, count your fingers and toes, and wait patiently for Mother's return. If the answer is "No, she's not coming back soon," you can observe the panic that sets in. That observation may explain what happens to you in later life when you don't get an immediate response from a person or a situation. You might tend to panic when panic is an inappropriate response in adult life. Finally, prepare yourself for the fact, in your imagination, that Mother has just gone through a trying experience and her manner has nothing to do with you. This prepares you for later freedom in letting people react to their own life situations, in their own way and in their own time, without taking things personally. This perspective allows the former closeness with Mother to continue. The danger in relationships comes with closing the doors and never reconciling the situations in a positive way . . . in your own mind. It is your perspective that makes the situation what it is.

Be sure to review the past in the present tense. That allows you to tune into emotions that are connected to the scene before your eyes. Be sure to trust what comes into your mind, even if it doesn't make sense at the moment. Keep asking yourself the significance of what you're getting. You may actually see pictures or just get an impression. You may find it works best to be quite logical by asking simple yes or no questions, as if you were taking a test in school. Would the answer be found in column A or in column B?

You can also learn to work with a pendulum to get yes and no answers. You can purchase a pendulum that has either a crystal at the end or a metal tip. Practice answering questions with answers you can verify. Observe which way the pendulum swings when the answer is yes and which way the pendulum swings when the answer is no.

Treat your own regression session as if you were making a personal film. Make choices along the way in the observation of your film. You are the screenwriter, the director, and the actor. Trust your fantasy first, but in observing objects in the room, as an example, you can make a choice about the color of the wall or the curtains at the window. That attention to detail only serves to get you to the real meat of the moment.

A very valuable moment in a regression session is the observation of the birth process itself. In a self-regression, ask yourself how it feels to be in the womb. Is it crowded, cozy, warm, or cold? Ask yourself if you know that you're going to be born. Some people are not aware of what lies ahead of them, and the beginning of the birth process comes as a great shock. You can be sure that later on in life, when that person is suddenly faced with events that may appear out of the blue, his or her reaction will be the same—a great shock. You can finally rewrite your birth survival script by asking yourself how you would have ideally been born into this world. You may not be able to change the reactions of other people in that scenario, however. If, as an example, you observe that when you were born, the doctors and nurses were tired and they were just going about their job in a perfunctory manner without any real excitement, you may realize that life brings in changes relating to outer circumstances where other people seem unenthusiastic. The important thing is that you have a choice about your reaction to their complacency. You can be enthusiastic about your new life even if the doctors and nurses are tired. The choices we make early in life are the same kind of choices we make right down the line.

One of the great values of understanding life from a different perspective comes from realizing that we cannot change other people! You cannot change the reactions of other people in the original scenario, of course. We can only change ourselves and our reactions to others. But that awareness can make all the difference in the way we lead our lives.

My greatest joy comes from knowing how a regression session can change a person's life. Sometimes feedback comes years after a session took place, but usually there is an instant feeling of lightness and a sense of relief. Doing a regression session is not a magic cure, but it is a first step to take in beginning to create a new life. After such a review, it becomes clear that we are the masters of our own destiny and that we have choices to make every step of the way along the road of life.

We can understand how judgments, anger, feelings of revenge, hatred, and any other negative reaction can create future problems for ourselves. Like a boomerang returning home to roost, those exact situations can return in future times or even in the present, to knock us down again. With new awareness, we begin to monitor our thoughts and reactions. Any tendency to judge, categorize, or label people and events makes them so in our mind. Those labels are the rocks on our paths that can trip us up over and over again, until we learn to walk around the rocks.

There is a saying, "What goes around, comes around." That is very true on both a productive level and a nonproductive one. Whatever good we do for others, or for ourselves, creates a plus sign on the wheel of karma. Negative thoughts, hurts, and pain create a minus balance. We may not be able to avoid immediate natural reactions, but we can always go back a short time after a painful event and review the situation that caused us pain.

Healing situations and people through the power of the mind is easier than we might imagine. It is sometimes more effective than trying to have a conversation with an antagonist. To take a look at situations from a different point of view may be all it takes to resolve a conflict or dilemma. Then, sending a quality of loving energy, asking for forgiveness, and visualizing a light around the situation may be all it takes to turn events around. Developing a new perspective is the key ingredient as a prelude to making conscious choices about our reactions and behavior. A new perspective naturally leads to the healing of past issues, if we choose to do so. It is, ultimately, up to each person to make a constructive choice.

It can be important to remember that we are preparing for our future lives even now. Every label and judgment is like putting a heavy weight on a situation. That weight will have to be lifted off at some point in time. It is better to do it now than to let it build in intensity. The tarot card "The Fool" carries an important message. The image on the card shows a young man with a knapsack on his back, gazing at the skies, and walking toward the edge of a cliff. It appears as though he is not watching what he is doing and will go over the edge. However, there is a small ledge just at the edge of that cliff. One meaning of that card is "There is always one more step to take."

This is true for everyone. Keep looking for that one more step in life, and ask for the inner light of the soul to shine on the path ahead.